HARRISON FORD

Also by Paul Honeyford

The Jam: The Modern World by Numbers
Michael Jackson: The Golden Touch

HARRISON FORD

—————————— A BIOGRAPHY ——————————

PAUL HONEYFORD

SIDGWICK & JACKSON
LONDON

To Katherine

First published in Great Britain in 1986 by
Sidgwick & Jackson Limited
1 Tavistock Chambers, Bloomsbury Way
London WC1A 2SG

ISBN 0-283-99320-0

Typeset by Rapidset & Design Limited, London WC1
Printed in Great Britain by The Garden City Press
Limited,
Letchworth, Hertfordshire SG6 1JS

Acknowledgements

Thanks to David Heaven, Adrian Costello, Mark Honeyford, Jane MacAndrew (for her infinite patience), Peter Hogan, Scott Dünbier (for individual assistance), my mother, and Billy Bragg, for telling it like it is.

Material used in this book was compiled from personal interviews and the following publications: *Blade Runner Souvenir Magazine*, *Return of the Jedi Collector's Album*, *Sunday Telegraph*, *Daily Mail*, *Raiders of the Lost Ark Collector's Album*, *Rolling Stone*, *Time Out*, *The Times*, *Playgirl*, *Starlog*, *Starbust*, *Sunday*, *Photoplay*, *New York Times*, *Prevue*, *The Face* and *Movie Star*.

The following books were also very helpful: *Skywalkin'* by Dale Pollock, *The Harrison Ford Story* by Alan Mckenzie, *A Journal of the Making of the Empire Strikes Back* by Alan Arnold and *The Making of Raiders of the Lost Ark* by Derek Taylor.

Finally, thanks to the Nathine-Walsh Collection for supplying photographs.

Contents

1

Opening Sequence

God created the world in six days and on the seventh George Lucas created *Star Wars* – and with it firmly stamped the word SUCCESS on the career of Harrison Ford, ex-bit player, supporting actor, aspiring carpenter, and man of distinctly well-defined ideas on life.

Ford has starred in five of the six most profitable films of all time, and he would have appeared in all of them if his guest role as Eliot's headmaster in *E.T.* had not been left out at the last moment. He has constantly sought to extend the range and depth of his acting abilities. Indiana Jones, the character he created, has burned its way into the public consciousness as perhaps only Sean Connery's portrayal of James Bond has succeeded in doing. Before the completion of *Indiana Jones and the Temple of Doom* a poll conducted by Paramount Pictures revealed eighty per cent audience awareness of the film before a penny had been spent on advertising. By 1984 Harrison Ford had become one of the most popular cinema actors in the world.

Although he seems to have carved himself a permanent place in the public psyche, Ford remains an essentially private individual who eschews the glitter and superficiality of Hollywood. Nonetheless, the low profile he adopts off-screen adds to outside interest in him and his films, and though he says of himself 'I tend to make boring copy', he remains one of the most sought-after and interesting characters in the modern acting school.

1

There are many reasons for his success and concomitant reclusiveness – not least the fact that, like his good friend Arizona-raised Steven Spielberg, he is a product of the mid-West and all its commonsense values. But his status in the film world owes little to the kind of fulsome rags-to-riches fable that Hollywood loves to attach to its self-proclaimed superstars. He has never been one to over-exaggerate his own abilities or importance in the industry. 'I don't take myself too seriously,' he has said. 'I've never been a film buff, and I've never studied or thought about other actors' work. Actually, I think I'm best suited to drawing-room comedy.' And he constantly belittles himself when faced with any over-effusive praise: 'I'm the un-star of the unexciting eighties' is how he frequently describes himself.

Despite his opinion of himself, Ford has a charisma, an on-screen presence, which harks back to the grand old days of Hollywood – the days of Gable and Flynn, of Grant and even of John Wayne. One of the reasons for this is his ability to dovetail his own personality perfectly with those of the flawed heroes which he so frequently portrays. Perhaps most importantly, everything about him is underpinned by a perfect grasp of down-to-earth values, and his performances are marked by an ability to see through pretence and pretentiousness in every guise.

Born on 13 July 1942, seven months after the horror of Pearl Harbor, Harrison Ford was given the name of his grandfather, a worker on the Brooklyn-area trams in New York City. He was the product of a typically mixed American background; his mother's combined Russian and Jewish descent was robustly complemented by that of his Irish Catholic father. The elder Ford, once an aspiring radio actor, had a successful career as an advertising executive in Chicago – not then prey to the polarization of wealth characteristic of the city today – and the family enjoyed a reasonably comfortable middle-class existence. Harrison Ford and his brother Terence enjoyed a fairly average upbringing in a fairly average American town.

Though his family had been involved in varying degrees with the acting profession – 'My grandfather was in Vaudeville for years, and my father was a radio actor. Still does voice-overs as a matter of fact' – it was not a career to which the young Ford immediately aspired. Never a great lover of Saturday mornings at the cinema, he much preferred playing around with cars and a few pitch-and-hit games of baseball. But he never really ran around in crowds and gangs, much preferring his own company to that of his peers. 'I was brought up in Chicago, Illinois,' he recalled, 'Average sort of childhood – no real surprise. Had no real idea what I wanted to do, later. I guess I was what you'd call a loner.'

Ford's father was raised to believe in the power of a dollar hard won and not so easily discarded, but young Harrison revealed little practical ambition. He seemed serenely unconcerned with achieving any success whilst at school, and though his teachers professed great hopes for him, they were more often than not frustrated. His tendency towards solitariness inclined him more towards a reliance on his own devices than on the advice and instruction of others, and though his marks were not abysmally low, they were disappointing. Fortunately for Ford, his parents were not the type to put undue pressure on their son. He seemed unlikely to fail to graduate from High School, and if he did not want to try for anything more significant, they felt he would just have to live with the consequences.

3

Perhaps becaue of this, Ford never formulated any concrete career aims. 'I never really knew what I wanted to do when I was a kid,' he observed. Even his extra curricula interests revealed no great passions. Despite his physique, he was singularly unimpressed by the school coach's admonitions that he should audition for the school teams. Nor did he reveal an early interest in the world of cinema. 'I never spent much time going to the movies,' he observed. 'At least not for the purpose of watching the film.' This youthful lack of concern with his future is an attitude he has carried with him into middle age. 'It's today that counts,' he has said, 'not what was yesterday or will be tomorrow. . . In a way, I still resist maturity. I like to play – fortunately my work is my pleasure.' And he has admitted: 'I was never really level-headed.' His childhood seems, by conventional standards at least, to have lacked a certain focus.

Ford's independence as a child taught him to trust his own judgement when faced with life's necessary choices. 'I'm not in favour of relying a lot on other people or on organisations and groups,' he told journalist George Haddad-Garcia. 'You have to find the touch yourself. In the end, you're the only one you can depend on. That isn't cynical or selfish – it's realistic.' This realism has helped to give Ford's acting a particular strength of purpose, and makes him a man who expects of others only what he expects of himself. Richard Marquand, director of *The Empire Strikes Back*, observed to Alan McKenzie: 'Harrison doesn't suffer fools gladly. If you don't know what you're going to do on the day, he gets a little confused and upset. But he's terrific as an ally, someone who understands the craft of being a movie-maker.' It is this coupling of the spirits of autonomy and co-operation which has consistently characterized Ford's approach to life as well as work, and has pulled him through some less than successful patches on the way.

Ford lacked ambition and academic application, but he was not inactive or lifeless as a youngster. He had a passionate and informed interest in cars. Visits to the local drugstore inevitably ended in an admonishment from the owner to stop reading the automotive manuals and magazines, and he took any and every opportunity to borrow his father's car – and those of his friends – to perfect his nascent driving skills. At one time he even considered the possibility of a future as a racing driver. Apart from the more practical school lessons – particularly woodwork – this was the only real career-orientated enthusiasm he evinced.

After graduating from High School, Ford followed the time-honoured course available to undecided American teenagers and went to college. A degree course in English Literature and Philosophy at Ripon College, Wisconsin, culminated in less than spectacular achievement, however. Following a 'total academic breakdown' – in his final year he was supposed to complete a thesis on the work of Edward Albee, but he found more interesting things to do – and a realization that the subjects he was studying did not offer him a massive spectrum of job opportunities, he dropped out of college just three days before his final graduation. 'I was expelled in academic disgrace,' he remembered. 'Only time I've ever been sacked from a production. Upset my mother and father, though – they'd already booked into a hotel for the graduation ceremony.'

Any feelings of relief at having escaped the academic system were quickly dispelled, however. Having recently married his High School sweetheart, Mary Harrison, Ford soon discovered that the reality of the outside world

5

concentrated the mind wonderfully. His academic *faux pas* had left him with no qualifications that could be used as keys to a successful career, and in any case he was determined to avoid the kind of nine-to-five jobs he saw so many of his friends being sucked into. So he decided to take a shot at acting. 'I didn't know what I was preparing myself for,' he remembered, 'and I tend to save my perseverance for the things I'm interested in. I didn't want to be an actor until I realised there was nothing else I wanted to do.'

This new career move was not quite the quantum leap into uncharted territory that it first appeared. 'I'd had parts in a couple of plays in college,' he explained, 'and so once I'd left I fixed up for a while with a Summer Stock company.' Performing at Williams Bay, on the shores of Wisconsin's Lake Geneva, he found the experience whetted his appetite for the profession and also for more exotic climes: 'When Fall came round, I tossed a coin for where I should seek my fortune, Los Angeles or New York, screen or stage. It was September and snowing hard in Wisconsin so when it came up New York, I tossed again until it showed Los Angeles.'

Typically, he wasted little time in executing his newly laid plans: 'I just took off with my new wife,' he told journalist Jan Iles, 'as I couldn't perceive of getting a boring nine-to-five job. I wanted to be an actor. . . California won as I thought I might as well starve to death in the sunshine.'

Little could the 22-year-old have known just how prophetic his words would prove to be. For the time being, however, the couple carried on regardless. On their way to fame and fortune in their battered, fully laden Volkswagen, they decided to stop off at Laguna Beach, a coastal resort an hour or so to the south of Los Angeles. At the local playhouse Ford, never one to miss an opportunity, managed to obtain a part in a modest production of *John Brown's Body*. Unfortunately, he quickly discovered that the repetitive nature of stage performance was not something that appealed – simply repeating the same role night after night smacked too much of the conventional grind he wished to avoid – and he began to question the wisdom of ignoring the toss of the coin. He decided that his own talents lay more with the discovery of subtleties of character often lost on a theatre audience, and began to toy with the idea of turning his attention to films.

There was also of course the increasingly pressing need to make a living to be considered. Theatrical performance may provide artistic fulfillment, but it rarely pays the bills, and Harrison Ford was beginning to run those up with unnerving, if unavoidable, regularity. After the irresponsibility of his college days, the fact that choices had to be made and money earned proved more demanding of Ford than he had envisioned. It was not long before he and his wife had used up what little savings they had. Something had to be done.

At this time, with the good fortune that was to surface at many important points in his career, Ford was spotted in performance by the *New Talent* programme scout at Columbia Pictures, who arranged a casting interview at the studio. Ford leapt at the chance. So, in December 1963, the year John F. Kennedy was assassinated and *My Mother the Car* adorned the nation's television screens, Harrison Ford descended on Tinseltown. It would be fair to say he did not take the place by storm.

On his arrival at Columbia's plush LA offices he found himself confronted with an image of the archetypal Hollywood producer: a small man chewing the butt of a large cigar as if it were necessary to the continuation of life itself. Behind him stood a man Ford described as a 'racecourse tout'. Both men indulged themselves in the time-honoured way by ignoring the aspiring actor whilst chattering away on the telephone for a good ten minutes.

'Eventually they asked my name, height, weight and hobbies,' he recalled, 'then it was, "We'll let you know if anything comes up" from the tout, and out I went. If I'd gone straight down in the elevator that would have been the end of it, but I decided to go to the bathroom for a pee. When I came out, the tout was jumping up and down in agitation, crying "C'mon, c'mon, he wants you". I don't know what changed his mind, but he gave me a contract.'

It took six months before the details finally came together and then, in June 1964, Harrison Ford signed with Columbia Pictures for seven years and $150 a week. Marlon Brando he was not, but at least he was getting paid to learn his chosen craft – or so he thought. He soon learned that things at Columbia were about as unfulfilling for a novice actor as they were at the rest of the lumbering studios of the time. It was a period of acute disorientation in the film industry. The upsurgence of rock and roll, and the success of movies such as *Rebel Without A Cause* and *The Wild One*, motivated the Hollywood gerontocracy to look to the recently moneyed youth market for its next bucketful of profits. Unfortunately, aged studio executives in expensive, ill-fitting suits rarely have their fingers on the pulse of a younger generation, and it soon became apparent they were trying to exploit a teenage market that had never really existed. Harrison Ford's participation in this short-sighted policy was to prove acutely embarassing, exacerbated by the fact that he belonged to the generation to which the corporate figures wished to appeal.

'I had to compromise myself stupid all the time,' he recalled. 'I hated all the publicity crap all the young actors and starlets had to do. I remember doing a publicity shoot of a beach party – I was in a jeep in swim trunks, surrounded by a mass of really dumb blondes. I only did it the once. From then on I told them to find someone else. And they did.'

From the beginning, Ford found himself at odds with a system grown fat on serving cold imitations to a captive audience. The manipulation of actors which was so characteristic of the industry at the time did not suit someone as opposed to regimentation as Ford. There were constant aggravations, mostly minor, but nonetheless totally unacceptable to both Ford and his autocratic employers. At one stage, the studio asked him to change his name to something less ostentatious. Ford refused. Never one to take kindly to others trying to dictate the way he should behave, he resolved to play a waiting game whilst avoiding the worst excesses of Hollywood's solipsistic industry. 'I realized right at the beginning that it would take me a long, long time to get what I wanted,' he said. 'But I knew that them that stuck it out was them that won. That was my belief then; it still is.'

The payoff was to take some time in coming, for his attitude, if not exactly revolutionary, did little to endear him to his immediate superiors. In the meantime, he had other things on his mind. In between submitting as little as possible to the Columbia studio system rules – compulsory jacket and tie at acting classes, daily attendance required, an office job in all but name – he bought a house near the Hollywood Bowl, and decided to occupy his time improving it to his own specifications. This was his first serious attempt at carpentry and woodwork, a craft which he was to come to love only slightly less than acting. Never one to be daunted his lack of experience of the job in hand, he joined his local library, borrowed all its relevant instruction books, and set to.

9

Soon Ford became adept at the craft, and he revelled in the demands it placed upon him. The flair for practical application he had revealed in his earlier interest in cars served as a firm foundation for this new interest. He imbibed any relevant knowledge he could acquire with a dynamic enthusiasm that confounded all who knew him. Aspiring film stars simply did not do that sort of thing! 'I submitted myself totally to the logic of it,' he recalled, 'It was a wonderful thing to learn – I could see my accomplishments.'

In the meantime, the possibility of accomplishment in the field of acting seemed to be rapidly diminishing. His film career remained in a coma, and appeared unlikely to revive for some time to come. The studio hierarchy failed to see him as having any great potential; he was overlooked with increasing and depressing regularity. Even the publicity photos in the studio casting folder were not replaced as frequently as they might have been, leaving an image in the minds of directors and producers of a terminally young man who, like Peter Pan, was destined never to grow up.

Harrison Ford's sojourn in the movie capital of the world was taking a less than dynamic course. Any possibility that a part might somehow drift towards him seemed to be baulked at every turn by those who in Ford's view, had least idea which end was up. It was a time of constant dissatisfaction, relieved only by his growing interest in carpentry, but he was honest enough to realize that his predicament was not entirely the fault of others. 'I was such a bad learner,' he told Alan McKenzie. 'I profit from experience. I think acting classes teach you how to act in acting classes. I've made an awful fool of myself on film a number of times as a result, but that's how I learn.'

Unfortunately, there was very little experience coming his

10

way at the time. And to add insult to injury, or vice versa, he had an accident. 'When I first arrived in Hollywood, he has recounted, 'every morning I'd drive my Volvo down from my home in Laguna Canyon Road, a very winding road. One day I thought I really ought to take more care, and reached with my right hand across to my left side to clip my seat belt on. I lost concentration and went slap-bang into a tree. 'I was very lucky to be alive. But I did look a dreadful mess. Fortunately it didn't affect my career as an actor at all – I didn't have any work at the time.'

The only lasting result of the incident was a four-inch scar that lay just below his bottom lip – not the stuff of which Clark Gable clones are made, but no one at Columbia seemed to notice. At times Ford felt he had not been given a fair chance, and he knew that if things did not happen soon he would be considered too old for the studio to spend any time – or money – on him. He could see the likelihood of a new generation of actors coming through to leave him caught in the no-man's land between the old guard and the young pretenders. 'I always saw other actors, younger than me, making it big,' he recalled, 'and I wondered if it would ever be my turn.'

Finally, in March 1966, the studio decided to test the talents of their 24-year-old star pupil. Ford still looked like an eager teenager which probably influenced the casting department in their choice of role. His performance is best described in his own words: 'I played a bellboy once, in a movie called *Dead Heat on a Merry-go-Round* with James Coburn. I said, "Paging Mr Jones, Paging Mr Jones". He said, "Boy!" and I said, "Mr Jones?" As you can see, it was big stuff.'

He had to adapt his name for the film's credits to read Harrison J. Ford, since the Screen Actors' Guild had informed him that there was an old silent-movie actor called Harrison

Ford – one famous enough to have his name on Hollywood Boulevard, in fact. He later discovered that the old man had died in 1957, and so he dropped the middle initial after one more film. Considering that *Dead Heat on a Merry-go-Round* was not the most auspicious of Hollywood debuts, it was no doubt a good thing that he changed his name even that small amount. The film quickly slipped into the long list of also-rans put out by the studios at the time. Perceived mainly as a vehicle by which they could put Coburn on the screen, and thereby prise the mighty dollar from the pockets of his not inconsiderable corps of fans, the film nonetheless failed miserably. It did not even generate enough interest to qualify as a disaster.

To say Columbia Pictures was less than happy with Ford's performance would be something of an understatement. He was called to the vice-president's office and torn off the proverbial strip once it became clear just what a dodo of a film it really was. 'He told me, "You ain't got it, kid",' explained Ford, '"First time Tony Curtis appeared in a movie, he delivered a bag of groceries. A bag of groceries! And I knew straightaway he had star quality. I took one look at him and knew he had it. You ain't." It was only years later that I realized he wanted me to act like a movie star and not a bell boy.' Ford's purist attitude towards acting sat uncomfortably within a business environment where artistic merit was not so much a dirty phrase as a completely foreign language. Once again, his career was frozen out by people for whom he had little or no respect.

Rapidly returned to the nether world of acting classes, Ford quickly realized that his own belief that a job worth doing was worth doing only if it was done well was not matched by the attitudes of the Hollywood star system, and so he continued

12

to pursue his outside interests. He soon found himself carrying out various small carpentry commissions for local residents, many of whom ironically were people he had previously had contact with in the film world, and in 1967 he even got himself employed as a general handyman-cum-carpenter at the Monterey Pop Festival. His manual work gave him a sense of satisfaction that his film career had yet to provide, and it afforded him a particular insight into the ways of the world. 'That's when I learned the correlation between money and respect,' he told Tony Crawley. 'Take a lot of money off people and they'll treat you with respect.'

After a year spent avoiding an interminable sequence of lectures on how to be a film star, he was finally given another opportunity to join the Tony Curtis School of Acting. After a small part in *Luv* – so small that he was not even credited on the cast list – he was offered another, unspectacular role. Columbia, having taken over the production of the Civil War drama *The Long Ride Home (A Time For Killing)* from Roger Corman, required a young, handsome supporting actor to play the part of a character called Lieutenant Shaffer. It was at least promotion. Along with George Hamilton and Glenn Ford, he put in his penny's worth – and pulled out a lemon. The only good thing about the whole affair was that this time he was not called to account for his performance.

By now, the whole routine was beginning to destroy even Ford's seemingly perennial optimism. 'It was horrible. Like a factory,' he recalled. He was not, therefore, dismayed when Columbia finally decided to let him go. When the option on his contract came up, he was once again called into the inner sanctum, this time to be informed that out of the goodness of their hearts the studio representatives would keep him on for a few more weeks. Ford, finally sick of being called 'kid' and 'boy' by people who, he felt, did not know the first thing about acting, informed them of a particularly creative use for the deal they were offering, and was sacked there and then. 'It was an odd time,' he told Tony Crawley. 'All the studios were making their biggest films in Europe, everybody in Hollywood was taking acid and smoking dope, and I was a baby actor getting nowhere.'

Unfortunately, by this time he was not even a baby actor any more: he was twenty-five years old, and most of his contemporaries had already secured productive careers for themselves. Ford was beginning to feel that opportunity had passed him by.

On the face of it, this was not the most opportune moment for him to make a stand against the system: his wife, Mary, was pregnant with their first son, Ben; and the house by the Hollywood bowl was not going to pay the mortgage by itself. But once again Ford landed on his feet. Three days after leaving Columbia, he was signed to Universal Pictures. Though he was again under contract and required to respond to the inhibiting demands of the studio system, he found his new home slightly more fulfilling than the last. Universal operated a policy using their contract players in the television series they produced, and Ford appeared in programmes ranging from *The Virginian* and *Gunsmoke*, through *The FBI* and *Ironside* to *Kung Fu*. The parts he played were similar – 'The guy who didn't do it' – and he began to realize that second-rate roles in TV usually lead only to more second-rate roles in yet more TV shows.

Though Ford did manage to whittle out a certain reputation as a solid supporting actor, nothing more fruitful was forthcoming. He decided that he had no real wish to become a Keenan Wynne for the seventies, and came close to giving up

14

acting as a nice idea but 'no cigar'. 'I thought I would wear out my welcome, and I would never get another chance at the kind of stuff I wanted to do,' he observed. However, in 1968 he was given a part in another film dealing with the American Civil War, *Journey to Shiloh*, which starred James Caan and Michael Sarrazzin. Cast this time as Confederate soldier Willie Bill Beardon, he found that crossing sides did not help much: he was shot early on in the story, and failed to make a great impact on the critics of the world. It seemed that there was to be little opportunity for learning anything new about the business of acting, and he found it difficult to take the initiative when given such insubstantial material to work with.

Universal, however, began to see a lot of promise in their new acquisition, though they did not seem to have a perfect grasp on how to develop it. In mid-1969 it was decided that Ford should be loaned out for a part in *Zabriskie Point*. The film's director, Michaelangelo Antonioni, had become notorious for his particularly idiosyncratic approach to filmmaking, and his 1966 movie *Blow Up*, starring David Hemmings – infamous because it showed the first glimpse of pubic hair on the British cinema screen – had cemented his unconventional and somewhat cultish reputation. In many ways *Zabriskie Point* was meant to be an extension of that earlier film, a statement on the ways of the world in general and of society in particular, but all in all it proved dyslexic in its various aims. The picaresque adventures of the film's protagonist may have been Antonioni's attempt to tune into the collective youth-consciousness of the time, but something went wrong. Perhaps fortunately, considering the way things turned out, Ford's role in the film was excised in the editing stage. It is difficult to ascertain exactly why his contribution was considered inappropriate, the best thing that can

15

be said is that he managed to escape with what little reputation he had acquired still intact.

Unseen forces continued to conspire to restrain the upward motion of the young actor's career. In 1970 he was offered a supporting role in the television film *The Intruders*, and then for his next film, the Elliot Gould/Candice Bergen feature *Getting Straight*, he was again loaned out by Universal – this time, ironically, to Columbia. The part was about as important as the wallpaper on the set. His experience so far had not been the stuff of which dreams are made. So, finally tired of the Hollywood carnival, Ford decided to turn down any parts which were not going to improve his career, and devoted his time to carpentry.

'I was being given tiny little spaces to fill, nothing where you could take the space,' he recalled. 'Maybe they were right, I probably wasn't ready. But I was getting older. You look at me now, I'm thirty-six, and everyone thinks I'm twenty-six. When I was twenty-six everyone thought I was seventeen. All soft and putty-like, but ageing fast on the inside, going crazy. I had to get away from it. Yet I had invested maybe four years and didn't want to give up. I still wanted to be an actor when I grew up. . .'

The various odd jobs he had carried out for friends and neighbours had increased his reputation as a handyman, and he was able to set up in business on his own. 'I taught myself carpentry from a library book and a Do-It-Yourself manual,' he recalled, 'and the very first job I did was build a one-hundred-thousand-dollar recording studio for Sergio Mendes in his backyard. He never asked me if I'd done such work before. And since he never brought it up, I never told him. Thanks to the manual, it all came out very well.'

The enterprise proved to be more immediately successful

than his acting career had, and within a short time he was able to set up his own contract building and carpentry business, employing other craftsmen to provide a more complete service. It was a significant point in his life. 'I taught myself acting the same way I taught myself carpentry,' he told *The Times*. 'You submit yourself to the logic of the craft. My approach to both jobs is entirely technical. What I learned from carpentry, above all, was the work ethic. I used to be very lazy, but now I find I can't enjoy myself when I'm not working.'

The success of the business also meant that, finally, the money pressures eased. 'Money was much more important when I didn't have it,' he recalled. In addition, the independence of his new-found vocation suited him perfectly. Apart from paying the bills, it also served to keep the artificial social life of Hollywood at bay. Ford spent much of his income on furnishing his house with early American period furniture, creating a refuge that could shield him from the excesses of outside. 'You wouldn't catch me in a disco unless I died and didn't go to Heaven,' he has said. 'I like people in ones and twos, not parties.'

Though he had decided to hold his acting career in abeyance for a while, he never once doubted his own abilities. 'I'm an optimist,' he told George Haddad-Garcia. 'Personally, I think that things tend to get better – your personal life, your career. There's no easy solutions, but if you hang in there long enough, things are bound to go right, and when they do, you'll be validated, and you'll enjoy the whole thing more deeply.'

Harrison Ford was in for a fair old wait.

2

The Writing on the Wall

Throughout the early seventies, Ford's carpentry business went from strength to strength. However, things did not always go as planned: during one job at the actress Valerie 'Rhoda' Harper's house, he fell off a ladder and broke his wrist. Though the bone healed without too many complications, it was an injury that recurred at regular, if infrequent intervals. Meanwhile, he was making a reasonable living which allowed him to view the acting profession from a refreshing, if slightly cynical perspective.

Ford no longer felt any great urgency to look for work in films, and a combination of pride and disenchantment left him unimpressed by the business generally. Any youthful idealism he had felt about the world of acting had been crushed by the cynical machinations of the dollar-obsessed Hollywood machine, but his *laissez-faire* attitude about his own availability – 'I was there if they wanted me' – was to prove a mixed blessing. Sticking rigidly to your principles is all very well, but when you are involved in a business that at best finds such principles a necessary evil, you can often do yourself more harm than good. At this time, Ford was written off as just another hopeful who had failed to make the grade, and the general consensus was that he did not have what it takes to fit in with a high-pressure, demanding business. But the fact that he stood his ground and refused to continue trivializing his abilities must have impressed someone.

He wasn't completely out of touch with the world of films, however – if only by virtue of the fact that he lived and worked in the Hollywood catchment area. And though he was no longer in the mainstream of the business, some people did seem aware that he was still alive. Unfortunately, the same could not be said for the majority of parts that came his way, but Ford now had the independence to wait for something worthwhile. Although he declined all roles with any hint of bellboys or the American Civil War about them, he finally agreed, in 1972, to take part in a film that would prove to be the first significant step on his rise to international success – the adept period piece *American Graffiti*. Appropriately enough, the project was about as untypical a Hollywood movie as could have been made at the time. It is a source of some wonder that it was made at all, for this was a period of retrenchment in the film industry, and declining audiences meant declining profits: no movie capitalist would risk a dime on something outside the rigid 'guaranteed blockbuster' mentality of the industry.

The project had been conceived by director George Lucas, a man whose sense of purpose and determination closely matched those of Harrison Ford. From his beginnings in Modesto, California, he had grown up with a passion for the cinema, convinced that his destiny lay in making films. It was a conviction confirmed for him at the age of fifteen when a serious car accident caused him to miss his High School graduation. Realizing that second chances are rarely, if ever, repeated, he spent two years at Junior College, and then attended the highly rated film school at the USCLA, from which he graduated in 1966 with several commendations.

In a sense, his adolescence paralleled that of Harrison Ford, though Lucas' academic disjunction was enforced rather than chosen, and it seems that the two men have certain formative experiences in common.

Both came from a similar family background – comfortable, middle class, without too many of the trappings of money – and exhibited an informed interest in cars. Lucas' great hero was James Dean in *Rebel Without A Cause*, and his accident may have owed much to an unconscious, if perverse, sense of homage. Ford never felt any such obsessive tendencies, and where Lucas sees life only in terms of film, he is wary of a commitment to any sort of 'ethos' of acting. Perhaps because of that, the two men find their attitudes and opinions strike a common and productive chord.

Lucas underwent a more typical, and nepotistic, film apprenticeship than Ford. After obtaining a job as a production assistant on the set of *The Rain People*, he struck up a working relationship with Francis Ford Coppola, the film's director. In addition to giving the young student the task of shooting a documentary film on the making of his movie, Coppola further recognized Lucas' talents by giving him practical and invaluable cinematic aid. Important people listened to Coppola's advice – a rare enough occurrence – and he was the prime reason for Lucas obtaining financial backing for his first independent feature film, the low-budget science fiction feature *THX 1138*. The project was conceived by Lucas whilst at film school, where he completed a shorter and even more depressing version, and was taken up by Warner Brothers and given wide enough distribution for the director to feel he finally had joined the Big Time. The film's clinical vision of life in the future contrasts sharply with the joyful grittiness of *Star Wars*, but it served then to highlight Lucas' skills as a director. Starting a policy he would follow through his career – prompted at first more by lack of cash than anything else – he went principally for unknown actors. In this first instance, it did not seem to help much. *THX 1138* failed, perhaps primarily because Lucas had to learn how to convey his intensely personal vision to others, but also because he was as yet unsure of his own attitude to the industry.

Ford refused to say at first whether he had seen *THX 1138* before he met Lucas, but he has since expressed admiration for the director's technique and sense of pace and style in the film. He did initially seem unimpressed by Lucas' in-school training, and the commitment to film as a theoretical as well as a practical medium was just a little too much for him. Ford had been at the hard end of the business for some six years, with nothing to show for it, and a jumped-up film student with pretensions to style might well have annoyed him intensely. Lucas' next project would change all that, however.

American Graffiti was to be a celebration of life and youth. Where *THX 1138* had painted the picture of a world that denied the spark of life, *Graffiti* tuned into one that exalted it. Lucas wanted to capture on film the indefatigable optimism that characterized the teenager of the Eisenhower era.

Unfortunately, though perhaps not unsurprisingly, the initial reaction from the film establishment was that the market for such a film was too small to justify investment. It seemed none of them could remember just what it had been like to be young. Lucas spent eighteen months trying to set up a production deal. He met with no success at all until he came across David Picker, President of United Artists, at the Cannes Film Festival, where *THX 1138* was being shown in the Director's Fortnight. Picker was sufficiently intrigued by the idea to provide enough money to develop a script. He also arranged a two-picture option deal that would include *Graffiti* and a space film Lucas was planning.

The first script that Lucas commissioned was by Richard Walters, a friend from USCLA. It was capable, but not what he had envisioned. Fortunately screenwriters Gloria Katz and Willard Huyck – who were to work again with Lucas on another Harrison Ford movie, *Indiana Jones and the Temple of Doom*, and whom Lucas had also known since film school – helped pull the script more into line with what he wanted. Unfortunately, after all this effort, United Artists decided not to take up their option on the film after all. Lucas was undismayed, however, and took the half-completed project to Universal, who gave the go-ahead with a budget of $750,000. As always, there was one condition: that Francis Ford Coppola, who had just had a massive hit with *The Godfather*, would be producer. Lucas agreed, knowing full well that he would be allowed significant freedom in the shooting of the film. Coppola was always more committed as a director by himself than as an overseer of someone else's work. It was the perfect working relationship.

By this time Harrison Ford had become aware of the project, but he felt no great urge to become involved. Lucas' zeal and absolute commitment often gave an impression of fanaticism from which Ford shied away, and it frequently looked as if the director would never get the project even halfway off the ground. No one quite realized the strength of Lucas' tenacity, or of his ability to get things done against the odds. However, Hollywood clearly recognized his talent. At one stage he was offered $100,000, a staggering amount at that time for a relatively unknown director, to take the helm of the film *Lady Ice* but he refused to be diverted from his personal vision. (This was a doubly wise choice, for *Lady Ice* bombed bigger than Enola Gay).

Lucas' determination and confidence in his own ideas and

23

abilities was to be the primary source of his later success, and was to impress Harrison Ford in particular. The director's professionalism and his belief in the power of film was a refreshing change from Ford's previous experience with the studio system. As Lucas told Alan Arnold: 'I like making movies. Hollywood is dedicated to making deals.' These are words which might easily have been spoken by Ford himself.

Harrison Ford's direct connection with *American Graffiti* began when Lucas brought in yet another old friend from USCLA, Gary Kurtz, to supervise the day-to-day running of the film, and the two of them asked Fred Roos, one of Coppola's old associates, to help with the casting. Lucas did not want any stars in the film, but he did want to create a team spirit, very much like that which can be found in a repertory company – a principle he was to carry through the later *Star Wars* films. Those involved in casting went around the theatre community therefore, and checked out the local talent. Whilst they were looking, Fred Roos remembered a young actor he knew from his days with Columbia Pictures, and told Lucas he would be just right for the part of Bob Falfa. Perhaps *Dead Heat On A Merry-go-Round* had not been such an unmitigated waste of time after all. Ford, typically, remembers the business of being chosen in a different, more prosaic light. 'When my wife, Mary, became pregnant with our second child, Willard,' he told Alan McKenzie, 'I realized my health insurance, that I'd had when Ben was born, allowed us to have a baby for about twenty-five cents a pound, was no longer in force. Because I hadn't made twelve hundred dollars in the previous year. So I had to make twelve hundred dollars to keep my health insurance. I said, "Well, I've got to do something". And a friend of mine, Fred Roos, was casting a George Lucas picture, and said I ought to be in it because it was going to be a big hit. It *was* in every way.'

An appointment with Lucas was arranged through Ford's agent, and though it was to be the turning point of the actor's career, he remembers the moment as being somewhat less than earth-shattering: 'I met George Lucas at an ordinary office interview,' he told Jane Goodwin. 'He was casting *Graffiti*, but I don't recall him at all from that first meeting. I don't think he even spoke. He sat while others talked. Later he said "yes", presumably. I had no impression of his being a *wunderkind*, nor of getting on particularly well with him.'

The director chose four or five people for each of the principal characters, and then auditioned them all on video tape, a process which has become common in Hollywood now, but which was relatively rare at that time. Ford was impressive enough not to have to go through the process. 'When I went for the interview,' he recalled, 'I wasn't there as a person who needed the job to put bread on the table. I had, for once, a real life behind me. When you're an out-of-work actor and you walk into an audition, you're an empty vessel. So this was a significant change in my personality. I had got my pride back.'

It was not simply his pride that Harrison Ford had regained, it was also his sense of purpose. The fact that things were generally healthier for him and his family allowed him to take a step backwards and see things for what they were, and for the first time he felt secure. Paradoxically, because of that, various tensions began to surface in his personal life – minor at first, but destined to become significant and overwhelming.

For the time being, however, things looked pretty good.

After the list of possibles was whittled down to a cast which included the names of many future film notables – Richard Dreyfuss, Ron Howard, Cindy Williams, Bo Hopkins and, of course, Harrison Ford – *American Graffiti* was ready to roll. Lucas pulled actors, crew and recalcitrant Hollywood moguls into some kind of line and on 26 June 1972, Harrison Ford's first film for two years, and certainly his best so far, started filming.

Lucas' determination to be as un-Hollywood as possible, coupled with an eager professionalism, conveyed itself to all concerned. Cindy Williams told Lucas' biographer, Dale Pollock: 'It was a great summer camp where we were all working against the clock and having fun.' This appealed to Ford in particular. He became notorious for his involvement in various shenanigans and practical jokes during the production – particularly in the company of Paul Le Mat and Bo Hopkins – and enjoyed himself thoroughly. His sense of confidence gave rise to a relaxed, carefree attitude that allowed his enthusiasm for the project to show through. He was nearly thirty years of age, but he acted like an eager twenty-year-old.

To create the impression of small-town America in the fifties, Lucas had to find a place where time had not exactly stopped, but had maybe gone out to lunch for a while. Although Lucas has always preferred to shoot in studios, he realized he would have to go on location to obtain just the impression he wanted. After some deliberation, he chose two small towns in Marin County, California – San Rafael and Petaluma. The locations appealed to Ford, whose dislike of big-city mores was well known. Though he was not involved in many major scenes – his part as Bob Falfa served primarily as a litmus paper for the other characters – he was always ready to provide exactly what was required. As the mys-

26

terious villain who talks big but who ultimately fails to cut the mustard – 'A sort of shit-kicker-cowboy-truck-driver type', he succinctly observed – his performance was perfectly gauged. With a part like that, he could easily have gone over the top and unbalanced the whole film but he did not, and Lucas in particular was impressed. Ford's name was filed away for future reference.

After four weeks of night shooting, enforced changes of location and increasingly pressing money problems, the film was completed and in the can – on time and on budget. At the viewing of a twenty-minute potpourri of scenes put together by Lucas for the end-of-production party, Ford turned to Cindy Williams. 'This is great!' he declared. And it was.

Before the film could be released, however, it had to be edited. Co-incidentally, whilst Lucas and company took that task in hand in Francis Ford Coppola's garage, Coppola himself was ensconced in his study writing *The Conversation*, which was to be Harrison Ford's next film. After battling with the studio over precisely who should edit what, Lucas worked unceasingly for several months to bring in the first cut of *Graffiti* at 165 minutes, which was still too long. Then his wife, Marcia, applied her renowned editing skills, and brought it down to just under two hours.

The first public showing was on Sunday, 28 January 1973, in the Northpoint Theatre, San Francisco. The film broke twice in the first ten minutes, the sound was not synchronized, and the audience thought it was the greatest thing they had ever seen. But the man from Universal hated it. And Ned Tannen, who had done an enormous amount to get the film off the ground in the first place, thought it was unreleasable, and insisted on various cuts. After much compromise – owing to the timely intervention of Coppola, who robustly

27

supported Lucas – the damage was limited to the dropping of three scenes: one in which Steve (Ron Howard) berates a teacher at the school dance; another in which Terry the Toad (Charles Martin Smith) is on the receiving end of a garrulous used-car salesman; and, finally, the scene in which Harrison Ford as Bob Falfa executes a passable improvised version of 'Some Enchanted Evening'.

This last scene was dropped for one of two reasons, depending upon which side of the fence you choose to stand: either Universal had budgeted only some $90,000 for music rights, and the cost of using the song would have smashed their limits; or the estate of the song's writers, Richard Rogers and Oscar Hammerstein II, did not feel the film was the right vehicle for the famed duo's material. The truth, as always, is probably a mixture of the two. Whatever the reason, on the film's re-release in 1978 the scenes were restored, and we were all treated to Ford's singing abilities. Sinatra he was not, but he passed muster.

On 15 May, at the Writers' Guild Theater in Beverley Hills, the re-edited film was previewed again, and again was rapturously received by everyone – everyone except, that is, Harrison Ford and Richard Dreyfuss, who crept out, embarassed by the acclaim they were receiving for their appearances on the big screen. For Dreyfuss it was the first time he had been seen in 70mm, and for Ford it was the first film of quality in which he had participated. It was not to be the last.

American Graffiti was an immediate smash. It went from strength to strength and received five Academy Award nominations, earning some $120 million in ticket sales. On an original investment of $1,275,000, Universal took over $55 million in rentals. It made Lucas a millionaire two or three times over, and it also made a significant contribution to Ford's bank balance. In a typically altruistic gesture, Lucas shared percentage points of the film's profits with his cast and crew.

This was a gesture which Harrison Ford found particularly appealing. He had already observed Lucas' astute head for business, and his film-making abilities – qualities which do not always go together – but this was something more. Nobody, but nobody in Hollywood gave away money when they did not have to. Lucas' generosity emphazised the extent to which he saw his actors as integral to his production, as opposed to ciphers to be instructed like befuddled infants.

Lucas' homage to American teen-dom and all it entailed was perfect in every detail. In Dale Pollock's biography of Lucas, *Skywalkin'*, Steven Spielberg called it 'the best story to come out of Hollywood since the late 1940s. . . It hit a chord of nostalgia because it was such a warm, backward nod. It was George's, mine, everybody's generation.' It was also Harrison Ford's generation, though he had never felt the same need towards the exaltation of youth that Lucas and, later, Steven Spielberg exhibited. For him, *American Graffiti* was just another job, however enjoyable, and though it did whet his appetite for more roles, he was perceptive enough to realize this one part did not necessarily herald his arrival in the world of big-time films. 'I was always real lucky,' he has observed. 'Things worked out more by accident than design from the very beginning.'

Following quickly upon the heels of *Graffiti*, Ford was offered a part in Francis Ford Coppola's *The Conversation*, once again through the intervention of the ubiquitous Fred Roos. Coppola had long had an idea for a story involving a professional wire-tapper, whose job of spying on others eventually leads him to a total lack of belief in any privacy in his life. He becomes laid raw by guilt and paranoia, recurring themes in Coppola's work, and eventually breaks down completely. For the lead role Coppola chose Gene Hackman. Ford's admiration for Hackman's work finally persuaded him to take a role in the film. It was a fairly minor part, acting as Robert Duvall's amanuensis, but Ford felt he could do something with it. 'There was no real part to play until I suggested we make him homosexual,' he observed. It was a curious explanation of his motivation; the character of Martin Stett may have been vaguely effeminate, at times even foppish, but any suggestion of homosexuality remained firmly in Ford's own perception of the character.

The film proved a reasonable success, garnering much critical praise and sending a trickle of film offers Harrison Ford's way once again. After a minor part in *The Trial of Lt Calley*, a television film, Ford was offered a role in yet another piece for television, entitled *Dynasty*. It had nothing to do with the later series, but was a typical tale of a Western family in the early 1820s, offering no real challenge to Ford's acting abilities.

Nevertheless, by 1976, Harrison Ford was finally beginning to receive the attention his talents deserved. His decision to use *Graffiti* to re-enter the film world was a shrewd career move in more ways than one. Not only did it highlight his particular, laconic qualities as an actor, and confirm his abilities in his own mind, it was also the beginning of his friendship with George Lucas. And neither man could possibly foresee the benefits that this relationship would bring.

3

A New Horizon

The disparate nature of Ford's acting career since *American Graffiti* unsurprisingly failed to set the film-world alight; no one was yet prepared to offer the carpenter his chance at the big time. However, the link with George Lucas was to prove to be the spark that his smouldering career so sorely needed. Since *American Graffiti*, Lucas had been carefully consolidating his position in Hollywood in order to give himself enough business as well as creative clout to bring his ideas to fruition. He had also kept in contact with Harrison Ford on a frequent if irregular basis. It was a combination of those two factors that was to bring success Ford's way, though not without its share of problems.

Lucas was to prove as idiosyncratic in his pursuit of success as Ford. Even today he has only grudgingly been accepted by the Hollywood establishment, and that more by the fact of his profitability than by his abilities as a director. Nobody in a position of power likes someone who subverts the system, as Ford had already learned.

The two-picture deal that Lucas had originally arranged with David Picker of United Artists – for *Graffiti* and 'this big sci-fi space adventure Flash Gordon thing' – had motivated him to pursue his ideas for the film that was to become *Star Wars*. After the many problems involved with the making of the first film, however, the studio declined to take up the option on the second, and it was only when *Graffiti* proved to be such an overwhelming success that Twentieth Century Fox stepped in and offered a $10 million deal for Lucas to make *Star Wars*. Such an absurd situation, going from a total lack of interest on the part of one studio to major and committed funding on the part of another, was not unusual in Hollywood, but Lucas saw the idiocy of it all. The wheeling and dealing involved in simply getting people to commit themselves to *anything* on the film was at odds with the director's prosaic but essentially commonsense approach to filmmaking. As soon as the opportunity offered itself, he would set up in business to provide himself with the entire range of facilities necessary to the making of a film. Any outside influence was to be eschewed; in the director's experience such influence invariably manifested itself as interference and impeded him in the achievement of his overall aim. His habit of sharing the profits also contributed to the sense of a small operation where everyone was treated fairly and justly – a feeling retained to this day, despite the size and wealth of Lucas' empire.

Harrison Ford loved it all. He rated Lucas highly as a director and innovator, but perhaps more importantly he empathized with his warmth and no-nonsense generosity. On the surface both men might have seemed a little cold and distant, but beneath the surface they matched each other stroke for stroke.

For the time being, however, Lucas spent eight hours a day for more than two years trying to pull together a final screenplay that encapsulated all his ideas. So grand was his concept that he found the one-film format was simply insufficient as a vehicle to convey the story of the Rebel Alliance and their fight against Evil, and so he conceived a nine-part series of which *Star Wars* was to be the first episode of the middle trilogy – this was Grand with a capital 'G'. When he finally had something coherent enough to show other people, Fox decided they wanted one or two well-known actors who could be used to promote the film. With typical independence, Lucas baulked at the suggestion, preferring as he did the idea of little-known performers playing the principal roles – perhaps because he felt he could mould them more to his own vision than he could the idiosyncratic egos of Hollywood stars – so he began to look towards the wider acting community for inspiration.

At first he turned his attentions to the local repertory companies, feeling that young theatre professionals could offer just the sort of qualities he was searching for. He was aware that much of the film-going audience might initially find his ideas for a space adventure a little too fanciful, and he therefore looked for individuals whose performance, might tie the film down and give it a resolute foundation. Unfortunately his initial foray did not work out, and he was forced to backtrack.

Harrison Ford had been aware of Lucas' plans for some time, for since his work on *Graffiti* he had been party to many of the director's ruminations, but he thought little about his own possible involvement with the project. Once again, however, the old camaraderie and complexity of inside-plays that was to become a characteristic of all Lucas', and to a lesser extent Ford's films, came through. 'George had let it be known that he didn't want to use anybody from *Graffiti*, the actor observed, 'Not because we'd disappointed him – a typical Ford understatement – 'but because he was writing a new thing and needed new faces. But old Fred Roos did it again. He prevailed on George to see me after he'd seen everyone else.'

33

'Old Fred Roos' did indeed do it again. Surprisingly perhaps, he seemed more aware of the possibilities offered by the success of *American Graffiti* than Lucas himself. In a curious way, the film had proved such a singular, self-contained success that the actors involved were fortunate enough to escape the stamp of Hollywood's own particular Mark of Cain – the dreaded curse of type-casting. Though it spawned many imitators – most obviously the television series *Happy Days* – the particular cultural nerve it struck in everybody meant that people associated *themselves*, rather than the actors, with the characters being portrayed.

In a peculiar fashion, more than any of the other actors perhaps, Ford had managed to distance himself from the character he had played. This was largely due to his down-to-earth attitude, and to the fact that he was not easily enamoured of the illusion of fame. He had taken enough hard knocks in the past not to fall for that particular temptation, and even now he only grudgingly accepts the fact that his work brings him more directly into the public eye. 'A lot of people recognize me,' he has observed, 'And some of them say something about it, and some of them don't. . . Basically I don't like it, because it takes me out of my favourite position, which is the unseen observer. It puts me in a position of being observed, which has no profitability whatsoever.'

It was this refreshing approach that Roos, in particular, recognized and since the completion of *American Graffiti* he had kept close tabs on all the principal actors, and pleaded their case at every opportunity. 'I had my finger on a whole range of hot people that I thought had a future,' he told Dale Pollock, 'though no one expected this cast to do what they've done.' Lucas himself seemed blissfully unaware of the success and corresponding potential of the people involved with the film, and he seemed prepared to look everywhere for his *Star Wars* characters except under his own nose.

In a sense his film-school training worked against him, in that he often tried to find some kind of radical alternative instead of simply playing it straight. It was an approach that had worked well enough with *THX 1138*, but Hollywood recognized different rules – and in Harrison Ford Lucas would find a man who knew to his cost just how those rules operated. Initially, however, it seemed fated that the two men would not come together on the project.

Yet once again, as on many occasions in Ford's erratic rise to success, both director and actor were blessed with more than a little help from Lady Luck. As Ford related in an interview in *Time Out*, 'The reason I ran into George Lucas again was because Francis Coppola's art director inveigled me into installing a very elaborate raised panel in his studio office. Now, I knew they were casting, and I thought it a bit coy to be around Francis' office, being a carpenter, during the day. So I did the work at night. Well, one day something came up, and I got stuck, and I had to work at the studios during the day. And, sure enough, that was the day George Lucas was doing the casting for *Star Wars*.

'There I was, on my knees in the doorway, and in comes Francis Coppola, George Lucas, four other captains of industry and Richard Dreyfuss. In fact, Dreyfuss came through first and made a big joke out of being my assistant. That made me feel just great. I felt about the size of a pea after they'd walked through. But weeks later, after they'd tested everyone else in the world, I got the part.'

The way Ford tells the story one might think that the man with the hammer in his hand and tin tacks in his mouth impressed more than the talented and eager Hollywood apprentices only because the casting team were desperate to fill the part. Needless to say, there is a little more to the story than that. Lucas had in fact teamed up at the Goldwyn Studios with Brian De Palma, who was preparing to direct the film version of Stephen King's *Carrie*, in order to assess the available talent. Commonly known as a 'cattle call', it was a process more often used in the casting of dancers for Broadway musicals than for finding actors for Hollywood movies; Lucas adopted the idea simply because it was cheaper than doing it on his own. In a sense, because he had been successful despite the Hollywood milieu, he did not know he was supposed to be spending money on all the wrong things. For the individuals being scrutinized, however, it was to prove a pretty unnerving experience as Mark Hamill, who gained the lead part of Luke Skywalker, observed to Dale Pollock: 'There were guys literally everywhere, in age from sixteen to thirty-five. They weren't going to let us read, you had to look right first. So I walked in, and they were both sitting there. Brian said "So, tell us a little bit about yourself", and I went through the litany. George didn't say anything. I thought he was Brian's gofer or something. In fifteen minutes it was all over.'

Hamill was successful, though he did not actually find out until Lucas rang him and told him to turn up for first rehearsals, but the process he went through – of never quite knowing what was going on – was typical of Lucas' approach. Harrison Ford, however, was fortunate in that he never actually had to read directly for any of the parts in the film. Because he was in the right office at the right time, Lucas asked him to read the male parts when he was testing various actresses for the role of Princess Leia. Ford agreed to fill in between wood panels, but he became increasingly disgruntled at not being offered the opportunity to test for the parts himself. Yet his professionalism in carrying out such a routine and unfulfilling task was such that even the notoriously unexcitable Lucas was impressed. Prompted even further by the diplomatic interventions of Fred Roos, the director began to realize that here was the proverbial gift horse he should not look in the mouth, and he began to see Ford as a distinct possibility for the part of Han Solo.

Ford has commented that he felt drawn initially to the part of Luke Skywalker – though with hindsight his darker quality would have clashed with Lucas' concept of his lead character – but it was the part of Solo that made a lasting impression. Solo is a maverick who breaks all the rules simply because they are the rules, but who also has a heart of gold. Who else but Harrison Ford could fit the part so perfectly?

The part had changed significantly from Lucas' original concept: in the first treatment Solo was a green-skinned reptilian monster, whose gills and noseless visage made his seven-foot physique only a little less enticing. Solo had also become an integral rather than a peripheral character in the drama. As Dale Pollock observed in *Skywalkin'*, 'Lucas wanted the sexual rivalry between Han and Luke over Leia to duplicate the classic screen jealousy of Clark Gable and Leslie Howard over Vivien Leigh in *Gone With The Wind.*' It thus became essential from Lucas' point of view that the principal trio of characters in the film were cast as a compatible unit. If Harrison Ford was to get the part he would have to complement Lucas' choice for the other two roles.

The casting process for Star Wars was reminiscent of that for *Graffiti*. The strength of that film lay in the power and subtlety of the ensemble playing, which was a quality Lucas wanted to recreate in *Star Wars*, though this time with a more immediate and linear plot. Interestingly, he had originally

37

thought that Solo might be played by a black actor, and at one stage he came close to offering it to Glynn Turmann. 'I didn't want to make *Guess Who's Coming to Dinner* at that point,' he told Dale Pollock, 'so I sort of backed off.' Many of the actors he then considered for the role were at that time struggling to build a successful career but went on to greater things, as they say in the movies – Nick Nolte and William Katt among them. Finally everything fell into place, and Lucas chose Mark Hamill, Carrie Fisher and Harrison Ford to play the three main characters. It is not clear whether he saw Ford as the equivalent of Gable or Howard in this particular *menage à trois*, but it was apparent that Ford's presence on screen was meant to provide order and stability amidst the action-packed, if carefully orchestrated chaos of Lucas' work. The director also knew from past experience that Ford would be of great help in fine-tuning the actual technicalities of the film's production.

Harrison Ford and George Lucas' working relationship on the set of *American Graffiti* had in a sense set the ground rules for their continuing involvement with each other. Lucas was a single-minded, if not autocratic director, and he expected both obedience and, perhaps curiously, independence of thought from his actors. In Harrison Ford he got just what he looked for. Ford was always aware of the physical demands of acting: 'If you and I were in a scene,' he told Alan McKenzie, 'and you were lit from back there, I'd be obliged not to move from here. It might be necessary for me to be here for the framing. . . That's the kind of restraint you're under, but I quite enjoy dealing with all technical problems. . . It's always weaving the bits together to make something as real as possible.'

Lucas was so dedicated to his idea of casting the three lead

roles as an interrelated trio that he had a second group –
Christopher Walken as Solo, Will Selzer as Luke and Terri
Nunn, a one-time Penthouse Pet, as Princess Leia – standing
in the wings in case any of his first choices could not, or
would not make it. Fortunately all accepted, but whereas
aspiring unknowns Hamill and Fisher leapt at the chance of a
major film role, Ford was convinced for more prosaic reasons.
'It was obvious what the relationship of the characters would
be simply by looking at the others,' he said. 'It was clear that
they were very contemporary and the situation very simple –
without meaning that in a derogatory sort of way. It was
simply straightforward, a clear human story. I mean, I didn't
have to *act* science-fiction.' This 'take it or leave it' approach
refreshingly out of step with normal Hollywood attitudes,
was perhaps the clinching quality that convinced Lucas of
Ford's suitability for the role of Han Solo, and which laid the
foundations for their future close relationship.

Not everyone thought this was a cast that was going to take
the world by storm. Francis Ford Coppola, a significant figure
in the careers of both Harrison Ford and George Lucas, told
Dale Pollock: 'I disagreed with George's casting but it was not
for me to say. I think had I been invited to be involved, as I
was on *Graffiti*, he would have had a different cast.' Coppola
was being a little disingenuous in his criticisms; he might well
have had a different cast, but then again, he would have had
a different film.

From Ford's point of view, what was clear in 1973, when
Graffiti was being cast, was that his reputation as an actor had
some way to go before it reached that which he had attained
as a carpenter. Lucas, for example, had considered him sufficiently 'unknown' to use him in the first place. But any man
who could spend much of a film acting next to a seven foot

two inch walking carpet, and not be upstaged, had to have something going for him. Of everyone involved in the project, he was the most aware of the kind of opportunity that was being offered, though he had no real intimation of just how successful the film would prove to be. *Star Wars* was the first time in my whole career where I could *take* space,' he said, 'not just fill it anymore. I just went ahead and did it.'

On 25 March 1976, the film that was irrevocably to change the course of Harrison Ford's life and career finally went into production. It was not an auspicious start. At every stage, from location filming in Tunisia – where the first winter rain the country had seen in fifty years thoroughly dampened, morally and physically, both cast and crew before they had even started – to the legendary, if unimpressive, Elstree Studios outside London, *Star Wars* struggled to take shape. Lucas may have almost overreached himself just getting the project off the ground, but the worst was yet to come.

From the beginning, the company found itself working against both time and money, forever chasing its own tail in ever increasing circles of despair. At one stage Mark Hamill was involved in a car accident and went through the windscreen of his car, necessitating drastic revisions to Lucas' shooting schedule. Nonetheless, the production was driven onwards by the sheer strength of purpose and determination of George Lucas' vision. And Harrison Ford contributed much to the vitality that would eventually shine through on screen. 'The only damper on the pure fun of that set,' he told Dale Pollock, 'was the almost unanimous attitude of the English crew that we were totally out of our minds.'

On reflection, it was an attitude not entirely without foundation. As on the set of *American Graffiti*, Ford chose to team up with various partners in crime – this time it was Carrie Fisher

and Mark Hamill – and tried his utmost to disrupt the mono-
tony and routine that threatened to engulf them all. On one
occasion, an ongoing Woody Allen-type skit, in which the
word Jew was substituted for various words in the titles of
popular songs, brought charges of anti-Semitism from certain
quarters. It was a charge which Fisher in particular – she is
half-Jewish – found ludicrous. That kind of inverted preju-
dice was grist to the mill for Ford, and he indulged his particular brand of on-set humour in increasingly bizarre fashion.
He might not have gone as far as he had on the set of *Graffiti*,
when he, Paul Le Mat and Bo Hopkins peed in the ice-making
machine, but nobody put their shoes on without first checking inside them when they knew Ford had been around.

Despite his penchant for lunacy, Ford never compromised
his professionalism, and he responded well to Lucas' promp-
tings: 'Very little time was wasted,' he observed in *Skywalkin'*.
'George didn't have an authoritarian attitude like many directors "Kid, I've been in this business for twenty-five
years, trust me". He was different. He knew the movie was
based so strongly on the relationship among the three of us
that he encouraged our contributions.' Ford did become notorious for standing in the middle of a scene and telling Lucas,
'You can type this shit, George, but you sure can't say it', but
he is quick to direct any possible praise about the role back
towards the director. 'I know many critics – fans too – say Han
Solo is based on John Wayne,' he has said. 'If that is so, it was
completely unconscious. I didn't know I was doing it, playing
it like Wayne at times. I just did. What was written down –
that's all George's genius. If I'm like Wayne in places, it's my
subconscious supplying something that's necessary.'

Despite Ford's protestations, the Wayne connection remains intriguing. In one of the best-remembered scenes in

the film – one often inexplicably cut out of screenings in some southern states in America – Ford as Solo shoots the bounty hunter Greedo in the space cantina. The juxtaposition of frivolity and almost cold-blooded violence is deftly observed, and, if it had not been for the appearance of some of the characters, the scene could easily have been dropped into any classic western and not looked out of place. The role of individual frontiersman who places his faith in one person only (in Solo's case, the wookie Chewbacca), can be traced back to such classic comic-book partnerships as The Lone Ranger and Tonto, even to Butch Cassidy and the Sundance Kid. In this instance, Solo grudgingly comes to love the human race, or at least a small section of it. Some might say the process resembles Ford's own life, and that may well be why he was attracted to the part in the first place: it allowed him not only space to move, but also an opportunity to explore part of his own character on-screen.

In a similar way, George Lucas saw something of himself in the way Ford portrayed the character. The role of Luke Skywalker may well have been a Lucas self-portrait, but Solo had the qualities he *almost* admired; everybody wants to be the bad guy with the heart of gold. Perhaps because of this, there developed a particular on-screen trust between the actor and director, which is exemplified in the story behind the scene where Solo, desperately pretending to be a storm-trooper in order to rescue the Princess, first stutters into the enemy radio, and then smashes it up in frustration. It was an improvised scene, suggested by Ford as the perfect way in which to show Solo's flawed bravery – and it worked. It is funny and gripping – again an acute blend of opposites – and reveals Ford's particular cinematic sixth sense which allows a scene to grow and then revolve around him.

Ford's portrayal of the 'sort of a free-enterprise small busi-nessman', as Lucas succinctly puts it, was clearly appreciated by the director who gave him, Fisher and Hamill two per cent of the film's profits to share – no small gift, considering that the film became the biggest earner in cinema history.

Lucas' generosity after *American Graffiti* had evidently not been uncharacteristic, although a subsequent incident hints that he was beginning to realize that he was now involved with very big money indeed. Before filming, Sir Alec Guin-ness, who played the old Jedi Knight Obi-wan Kenobi, re-putedly offered an extra quarter of a per cent of the profits to take part. This was never put in writing. After the powers that be saw just how profitable the movie was going to be, the extra amount was conveniently forgotten. *Star Wars* may have given rise to a sense of camaraderie unusual by Hollywood standards but, well, business was still business.

What was perhaps most important of all the things con-cerned with the project was that the chaos involved in the fil-ming strengthened the close professional and personal re-lationship between Ford and Lucas. 'We worked together on it,' observed Ford. 'I really like working with him.' He is quick to point out that 'George was always ready to help with the Solo part, changing phrases that weren't comfortable and adding various bits'. The freedom allowed him by Lucas to contribute ideas to the story was a welcome novelty; his pre-vious experience had been to be more or less dictated to by others, often with no idea of what was supposed to be going on. This was something new, and he liked it: 'I don't just want to walk through a scene making all the right moves. I like to put in my two cents' worth.'

Ford was also quick to take advantage of the fact that he was working with Sir Alec Guinness, one of the most accomplished and respected members of the acting profession. At first he felt unusually nervous. 'He gave me many sleepless nights,' he has observed. But he was soon put at his ease, and he learned many techniques of expression and performance from the great man. Guinness was not one to belittle his own accomplishments, however. Ford noted how he 'preferred' the title *Sir* Alec. But he was always generous, even paternalistic towards the younger actor. It was an experience Ford revelled in, and it gave him a confidence about his ability that he was to carry through his career.

If Harrison Ford's participation in *Star Wars* did cause any problems, it was not anything to do with the film-making process. He had been so indifferent to the world of acting that, prior to reporting for filming, he had arranged to do some carpentry work on the actress Sally Kellerman's house, intending to return after a few short days on set. Unfortunately, success being what it is, he still has not finished the job. 'We knew he'd get his big break one day,' noted Ms Kellerman, 'but we never expected it to happen right in the middle of a paint job in our kitchen.' Thanks to *Star Wars* Harrison Ford, jobbing carpenter, now seemed a thing of the dim, if not too distant past.

The philosophical and refreshingly realistic attitude towards filming that the film engendered in both Lucas and Ford can be observed in the director's own feelings towards his creation. 'Whatever little event in history that *Star Wars* is going to be, at least it's done,' he told journalist Paul Scanlon. 'If people want to look at it, they can. . .' And they did. On 25 May 1977, *Star Wars* opened in thirty-two theatres across the United States to immediate and overwhelming acclaim, catapulting a rather bemused Ford and colleagues to stardom. George Lucas was so unsure of the film's reception that he

44

ran off to Hawaii for a holiday, but the cinema-going public harboured no such doubts. The film made more money than any other in history, dominated television news programmes and magazine articles, and changed many people's lives. Three months later it had grossed over $100 million, and it went on to garner some $600 million in sales. Harrison Ford had struck the Big Time.

The profit share that Lucas had generously given his lead players amounted to approximately $200,000 in Ford's case, enough to keep the wolf from the door, and to allow him significant flexibility as to where he acted next. It also made him a household name. 'Just like the movies again,' he observed. 'An overnight success, albeit that the night was fifteen bloody years long. I don't have as unique a physiognomy as Carrie or Mark, so I'm much less recognized in the streets, which I'm pretty happy about. People are usually very nice, though, because the film is broadly accepted. And it's opened up a lot of doors for me.'

Realizing this, Ford was at pains to acknowledge the extent to which his wife in particular had been instrumental in his success. 'I owe everything to Mary,' he explained. 'I'd never have accepted *Star Wars* when I hadn't been in front of a camera for three years without her advice. She wasn't just beautiful and kind. She understood my problems and helped me.' It seems ironic that the film that was perhaps the crystallization of their supportive relationship was also to spark off the success that was ultimately to cause them to drift apart. Perhaps it is because of this that Ford, in typically ambivalent fashion, maintained that the film 'wasn't a personal success, but the success attributed to it rubbed off and gave me a job. I didn't anticipate that kind of good fortune, it was *crazy*. . .'

45

It is hard to imagine in what way the film could be said, in acting terms, to be a failure for him, but this early evidence of an urge to self criticism was to become characteristic. Ford fell into the habit of belittling his own efforts soon after committing them to celluloid, which is perhaps the luxury only of the truly successful. Yet, however inconsequential he tried to make his own efforts sound, *Star Wars* was the fulcrum of Harrison Ford's rise to stardom. After three years of building New American kitchens and plush, panelled interiors of Hollywood offices, Ford had decided to take one last swipe at acting. If the film had flopped so, finally, would Harrison Ford the actor. Now, however, Hollywood was chasing him. It was time to take acting seriously once again.

4

Incidentally. . .

After the huge success of *Star Wars*, it looked as if Harrison Ford would experience little trouble in choosing which step to take next. If anything, he could expect a whole range of roles to be offered to him in the light of his acclaimed portrayal of Han Solo. But unfortunately things did not work out quite as easily as he had anticipated.

Hollywood has perhaps the most glaucomic vision of any profession, and as Lucas' creation stormed to greater successes around the world, the film capital's producers and money men worked feverishly to duplicate not so much its popularity as its profitability. Lucas became involved in litigation with the makers of *Battlestar Galactica*, because he felt that of all the new material to follow *Star Wars* it at times paralleled his film just a little too closely. More than anything, Lucas wanted simply to guard the reputation of his work, and, the cynical might observe, the merchandizing opportunities opened by it.

Harrison Ford met with a similar problem. Imitation may be the sincerest form of flattery, but most of the offers that came his way did not impress him. 'By and large, every time I'm in a successful film, I receive a whole bunch of material, imitations from people looking to get the same job done, and I don't read those', he said. 'Then there's another level of stuff that comes in, and I simply do not agree with the intention of what those people are after. That's the second biggest body of rejections. . . I don't necessarily want to be taken seriously, but I would like to do some serious roles. Unfortunately, one must be thought of as serious before one is offered serious roles.'

Ford was now in a position whereby his name alone would guarantee a certain audience, and that brought with it a measure of influence in terms of the deal he could negotiate. Whereas before he had had to accept a fixed fee for his performance, now he could ask for a percentage of the profits. But first he had to find the right part.

To his disappointment, it took some time before he found a project in which he felt able to participate, and even when he did it was not destined to be the greatest film the world had ever seen. 'I saw the success of *Star Wars* as an opportunity to diversify, and to get work I would not otherwise have had a chance at,' he told Alan Arnold. 'I went from that to a picture called *Heroes* with Henry Winkler and Sally Field, and directed by Jeremy Kagan. I played a Vietnam veteran living in his old hometown, a farming community in Missouri.' The plot of the film sounded like something off a Bruce Springstein album – all mom 'n' pop Americana, with a dash of The Only War the USA Ever Lost' – and it seemed to fit uncomfortably with the Hollywood scheme of the time. The large studios were turning their attention more and more towards profit-generating blockbusters, ironically partly initiated by *Star Wars*, yet *Heroes* seemed singularly out of place in terms of scale and subject matter.

Heroes was conceived specifically as a vehicle for *Happy Days* star Winkler, who had become as dissatisfied as Ford with the cosy, ego-massaging atmosphere of Hollywood. Like his co-star, he was looking for an opportunity to prove to others just how far the range of his on-screen talents extended. In the film Ford was again cast as the engaging side-kick with a heart of gold, though typically he had a few suggestions to make as far as character development went. But this time it simply did not work. The part was just too small for him to play. Ford's role as Han Solo had increased his popularity as an actor, and had intensified the expectations that his presence on-screen engendered. The part of Kenny Boyd in Winkler's film simply did not match what the public now wanted to see.

On reflection, it is difficult to understand why the role appealed to Ford in the first place. He had enough offers to choose from, after all. 'I had a chance to create a completely different image from Han Solo,' he has explained. 'I knew that *Heroes* would be very quickly released, and would show me in something totally different, and thus give proof of my versatility.' It seems an unusually short-sighted point of view from a man known for his clear thinking, and for knowing just what he wants out of life. The part did not so much show Ford's versatility as indicate that he was a little lost for ideas as to where he should go next. Reading between the lines, it may have been because he was having difficulties in his relationship with his wife that he felt the need to immerse himself in work. It was, unfortunately, not a solution that would work for any length of time.

The film proved a box-office failure. It disappeared without making much of an impression on anybody, which was not really that surprising. It was not a typical Hollywood product, and its background, the Vietnam War, pre-empted Hollywood's coming obsession. Perhaps people were not ready for that kind of approach.

Ford shrugged off any disappointment he may have felt. He felt he was always storing up not only invaluable experience, but also the power eventually to establish the freedom to act when and where he wanted. However, he could be seen to be curiously unconcerned with the success of this particular film. Though he tried hard to rationalize his involvement in terms of the experience it offered him, it did little to further his career. He did develop a friendship with Winkler, whom he regards as 'a real professional – more talented than his TV series shows him', but little else of note came to light. *Heroes* remains a curiosity.

Soon after finishing *Heroes*, Ford's old friend Fred Roos once again came up with a suitable part for him to play. It was only a ten-minute cameo performance, but it was to go a long way towards bringing Harrison Ford back to the attention of the film industry and its financial backers. Out of the sequence of films in which he appeared in the two-year period following *Star Wars*, this was to prove the only one with any lasting quality. *Apocalypse Now* had, curiously enough, been dreamed up by George Lucas in association with fellow USCLA student John Milius – who was later to direct such classic examples of right-wing dogma as *Red Dawn* – even before Lucas had filmed *THX 1138*. He had tried to resurrect the idea whilst working on the screenplay for his space adventure, but after various contractual differences of opinion he decided not to pursue the project. The rights to the movie now lay with Francis Ford Coppola, who chose, however, to make a spectacular anti-war movie where Lucas had envisioned a 16 mm documentary-style story of one man's inability to live with the world as it was. Coppola spent over two years and $36 million dollars putting his ideas on the screen, almost destroying himself and everyone else in the process. The film became a legend in Hollywood circles for the way the intensity of the subject matter was almost perfectly matched by that of the production schedule. Into this snake-pit wandered Harrison Ford.

Because he had known Coppola from the time of *Graffiti*, and had already worked for him on the adept and intelligent *The Conversation*, Ford thought he knew what to expect. He could not have been more wrong. At times it felt like the cast and crew were fighting the Vietnam War all over again – and losing. He was not required for any sustained period of acting, but he did have to go on location in the Philippines.

Here, the curse of Ford's film-making career struck again: during his location filming he contracted a virus, which was at first believed to be dysentry, but which fortunately cleared up after a couple of days. Suffice to say, he had a rather unsettling time.

Things were not all bad, however. Throughout the filming Ford managed to retain his sense of perspective about what really mattered, and he was able to indulge in a whimsy of his own. 'I did a cameo role in Coppola's *Apocalypse Now*,' he told Alan Arnold, 'playing a colonel in Army Intelligence, a quirky kind of character. Because the character had no name in the script, I called myself Colonel Lucas – a little in-humour.' It was in fact more than that; it was a deft and affectionate tribute to a man Ford recognized as being instrumental not only in the development of his career but also of his life in general. 'I'm only in the one scene,' Ford remembered. 'What we call the laundry-list scene – it told the audience all they wanted to know about the rest of the movie. When George saw it, it was halfway through the scene before he realized who I was, and that was just the way I wanted it.'

Apocalypse Now, perhaps contrary to most people's expectations, proved a substantial public and critical hit. In association with *The Deer Hunter* and, to a lesser extent,

Coming Home, it steered the American people to an acceptance of the Vietnam War as an important and moving part of their history. It was evocative and immensely powerful, cinema at its very best, and Harrison Ford was proud to have played even a small part in its creation.

The film was important to Ford for other reasons, however. Whilst shooting his little insert on location, he met a production assistant called Melissa Matheson, who was to go on to become a successful screen-writer with films like *The Black Stallion*, *The Escape Artist*, and the phenomenally successful *E.T.* to her credit. The two developed a more than professional relationship, though it was to be some time before they could proceed in just the fashion they wanted: Ford was still married, and he certainly was not a cheating husband. But it was nonetheless a fateful meeting. The actor's home life was somewhat disrupted at the time, and he appears to have felt that here was a woman who, because she was as much a part of the film industry as he was, understood perfectly the peculiar kinds of pressure he was under. He was intrigued. For the time being, however, he turned his attention back to the job of acting, although this time he may not have felt the need to submerge himself in his work.

After his involvement with *Apocalypse Now* and *Heroes*, Ford's career continued in a similar vein. In 1978 he was cast in *Force Ten From Navarone*, effectively taking over the Richard Harris role in *Guns of Navarone*, though everyone was quick to deny it. Taken, as was its precursor, from an Alastair Maclean novel, the film told the tale of a team sent to assassinate a German spy in Yugoslavia. As Lieutenant Colonel Mike Barnsby, an American ranger who is effectively cashiered into taking part, Ford carried on his sequence of military promotions on film. It was becoming clear that, for producers and casting agents at least, he was beginning to be regarded as the perfect heroic support for the lead. He was also seen as the archetypal American hero himself – bruised and a little battered, but determined to succeed against any odds. For Barnsby, winning is not everything, it's the *only* thing. Although Ford's attitude to life was not quite as mercenary as that, it did seem he was being cast in parts which made use of certain aspects of his personality.

Director Guy Hamilton's concept of *Force Ten* indicates that Ford was regarded as something more than just a walking military clothes horse. 'It's a rip-roaring adventure told in 1978 terms,' he told journalist Iain F. McAsh, 'Excitement all the way, and you've got all the twists and surprises that Maclean always puts into his novels. Force Ten go in like a gale, flattening everything before them – but what intrigued me was that it's more than a war picture: we've got five marvellous characters who absolutely hate each other. . . Here are these five idiots let loose in Yugoslavia as walking disaster areas. It's the characters who are so interesting against a war background and this great stark scenery.'

It was this refreshing concern with character, carefully married to adventure and excitement, that attracted Harrison Ford in particular. The film was not to be solely concerned with the glorious fighting man showing off his prowess: the intention was to explore how diverse characters are able to deal with the tensions that arise in such a situation. With that in mind, Ford saw the film as reinforcing his growing status as an actor. As ever, he was astute enough to appreciate the advantages his role would yield. 'It's fun to do these supporting roles because they're good character pieces,' he commented. 'The problem is that they don't usually write character parts as the leads of the movies. Unfortunately, you can't always play the supporting roles because of the complicated vision that people in this industry have. Hollywood only really takes notice when you're being paid the money and given the billing that a "Lead Actor" gets. That's why *Force Ten From Navarone* was important for me to do. Its cast was a package of big names, which included me.'

So Ford was beginning to realize that it was time to branch out a little, and bring himself to the attention of Hollywood's casting elite. However much he might dislike the way the film industry operated at times, he could not deny it forever. If he did, he simply would not meet with success at all. *Force Ten* might just be the means to break through.

It seemed that Ford had decided to adopt a new, hard-nosed approach to his career. The correlation between money and respect that he had learned during his carpentry apprenticeship seemed applicable to the world of film, and he was determined to exploit this, too, to its fullest advantage. 'It's a tool this so-called stardom,' he told Mike Munn. 'It means I have the opportunity to work a lot more and have more say about the films I do.'

In choosing *Force Ten*, Ford knew that he was beginning to slip towards the treacherous sands of typecasting, but felt that the benefits far outweighed the dangers. He was content to continue learning his craft. 'Acting is like carpentry,' he observed, 'It all comes down to detail.' Though the film required that he spent some time away from home, the company of so many fine actors offered a particularly instructive environment. Amongst such notable and seasoned campaigners as Edward Fox, Robert Shaw, Alan Badel, *et al*, Ford held his own extremely well, avoiding the temptation to overplay his part, or steal whatever thunder he might from his co-stars.

Fox, Shaw and Badel brought with them a particularly

English approach to the task of acting. The vague disdain that English actors seem to have for the cinema – a disdain that can be traced back to Laurence Olivier's great declaration on the set of *Wuthering Heights* that, 'The trouble with this pathetic medium is that it can not sustain great acting' – often brings a singular quality and depth to the parts that they play. Ford, raised solely in the Hell's Kitchen of Hollywood film-making, learned a great deal from the casual, relaxed attitude of his co-stars. 'Never take things too seriously, my boy,' Fox reputedly told Ford. 'Be serious about it, but don't take it seriously. After all, it's only a movie.' It was an admonishment that Ford seemed to have taken to heart.

It was clear that he saw the part of Mike Barnsby as a means to an end, the opportunity to see just how far he could push his abilities. 'He (Barnsby) is a man of real capacity,' he told Tony Crawley. 'He flies, he fights, he's got brains, but everything works against him. At the last minute he gets Robert Shaw and Eddie Fox tacked onto his mission, so there's a lot of adversity in the relationship between them, until he begins to need them and they begin to need him – a nice kind of continuity of cross-purposes that becomes established and finally resolved. An interesting character. I think it'll work. I never know . . . I never really know. I just know how much better *if*. . . That's the worst part, absolutely the worst part. . .'

This quality of constantly questioning his own performance and striving for something better has always characterized Ford's approach to his work, but, unfortunately, in the case of *Force Ten* the doubts seemed to be more than justified. The part proved less dynamic and taxing than he had initially supposed. Indeed, interviewed on set by William Hall, he replied, 'Okay, I'll try and think of something

positive to say about this location. . . No. . . But give me time.
. . I tell you, the hardest thing we have to do on this film is get
up in the morning.'

Ford had discovered that, despite everyone's professed
good intentions, Lieutenant Colonel Barnsby was more a fil-
ler role than a central character. He was expected simply to
look good, rather than to contribute anything significant to
the production. This was unfortunate for, as always, he had a
lot of ideas of his own on how best to play the part.

Harrison Ford's dissatisfaction was reflected in the critical
disfavour which the film received on its release, and, in the
light of that, Ford modified his public stance even further.
'Mike Barnsby was one of those macho, tough-guy roles that
everyone *thought* I should be doing,' he told one interviewer.
He was even more candid with another: 'It was a job I did for
the money – and I was lost because I didn't know what the
story was about. I didn't have anything to act. There was no
reason for my character being there. I had no part of the story
that was important to tell. . . It wasn't a bad film. . . But it
wasn't the right thing for me to do.'

It is unfortunate that Ford considered it necessary to explain away his involvement in such a fashion, for the film deserved better reviews, and his performance in particular was
nicely judged. His attitude may have owed more to
traditional Hollywood values than he would care to admit:
following the overwhelming success of *Star Wars*, it would be
reasonable to suppose that he found it difficult to function in
a supporting role. After all, once you have saved the Rebel
Alliance, the adventures of Mike Barnsby pale into insignific-
ance. However, Ford did retain a refreshing sense of perspective. 'I just want to keep on working,' he told Tony
Crawley, 'preferably in scary roles, something I'd never

Ford in *A Time for Killing*, 1967 (*Columbia Pictures*)

With Camilla Sparv in *Dead Heat on a Merry-Go-Round*, 1966 (*Columbia Pictures*)

Ford looking slightly uneasy with the Concho County Comanches in *Journey to Shiloh* (*Universal Pictures*)

Studio shot taken at the time of *American Graffiti* (*Lucasfilm Limited*)

Harrison Ford with Chewbacca in *Star Wars* (*Lucasfilm Limited/Twentieth Century Fox*)

Ford as Han Solo in *Star Wars* and, below, with Mark Hamill who
played Luke Skywalker (*Lucasfilm Limited/Twentieth Century Fox*)

In *The Frisco Kid*, in which Ford co-starred with Gene Wilder (*Warner Brothers*)

Ford was able to use his carpentry skills in *Heroes (Universal Pictures*

Publicity shot from *Hanover Street* with co-star Lesley-Anne Down (*Columbia Pictures*)

Ford returns as Han Solo in *The Empire Strikes Back* (*Lucasfilm Limited/Twentieth Century Fox*)

A romantic interlude with Pricess Leia, played by Carrie Fisher (*Lucasfilm Limited/Twentieth Century Fox*)

imagine for myself. Otherwise you start churning out bullshit – and that lives on long after you've flushed yourself. It's still there, forty feet high and sixty feet wide, screaming, "Bullshit, bullshit, bullshit! This guy was a fraud!".' Harrison Ford certainly is not that.

At this time, other unwelcome pressures were brought to bear: his increasing popularity was putting greater strains on his family life. 'We have two boys, aged nine and seven,' he told Mike Munn. 'They're still at school at the moment, but I was lucky enough to take them, and Mary, to Yugoslavia with me when we were shooting for this film. But it's difficult to pull them out of school for a time at this stage in their lives. I hope in a couple of years my family will be able to travel with me all the time.' Ford may have been fooling himself a little. He had already met Melissa Matheson, and he and Mary had grown too far apart to go back. The truth was, perhaps, too hard to face at that time. His increasing workload continued to keep him away from the family, and for the next few years he and Mary were separated continually as they had been in the recent past. 'Hell, I've been making this film for the past six months,' he recalled. 'Before that I was in the Philippines making *Apocalypse Now*, before that I was in England making *Star Wars*. It seems like I've only been home for a couple of months in the last couple of years.'

Even the completion of *Force Ten From Navarone* did not offer Ford any opportunity to take time out, however. He was soon off again, this time back to England to film *Hanover Street* for director Peter Hyams. The film was envisioned by Hyams as a remodelling of Noel Coward's classic *Brief Encounter*. It transposed the story to World War Two – Harrison Ford must have felt he had been permanently drafted – it brought in a cross-cultural and more physical element to the central

57

relationship, and tried to add a sense of adventure that the original lacked. It was to fail, and Harrison Ford seemed a little evasive about his involvement. 'It seemed an interesting project,' he told Alan Arnold. 'It was a love story . . . and I felt that a love story was something I had to do to become an all-purpose movie actor. But it was *another* World War Two picture. I played a bomber pilot forced down behind enemy lines, and spent half the picture in Nazi uniform. Nevertheless, there was top star-billing with Christopher Plummer and Lesley-Anne Down. Yet, you know, the billing didn't bother me any more. Once I had achieved the billing with *Force Ten* I could give that up as a plus factor.'

When pushed, Ford has revealed a more disillusioned attitude. 'I don't even like to think about *Hanover Street*,' he told Alan McKenzie. 'The director and I did *not* get along. I've never seen the film. . . My motivation for doing Hanover Street was because I had never kissed a female human being on the screen before. The characters I played were totally sexless, and here was a movie that was being touted as a romance. That was a clear, obvious reason for doing it. . . There are a lot of other reasons, which may or may not have been the right ones for doing it.'

Some of those reasons must have had something to do with his disintegrating home life; others with the fact that he had been offered the chance to carve out a career for himself, and he was going to use every opportunity that came his way. It is evident that *Hanover Street* was not Harrison Ford's favourite project, but it should be remembered that he had never yet been completely satisfied with any project with which, he had been involved. He was actually a little ungenerous in his criticisms of *Hanover Street*, which had its moments, even if it did lack a certain depth and exposition.

After *Hanover Street*, Ford jettisoned the military persona and donned chaps, six-guns and a stetson to play Tommy Lillard, cowboy, outlaw but ultimately all-round good guy. One day he was going to have to play a *real* 'baddie'. 'I did *The Frisco Kid* with Gene Wilder, directed by Robert Aldrich,' he told Alan Arnold. 'I'm happier about that experience than the others I have mentioned. Working with Aldrich was marvellous. I play a kind of bank robber cowboy character, a rough guy in the Old West, a character that contrasted well with Gene Wilder's Polish rabbi. Together we make the journey from New York to San Francisco, so it's kind of a road picture.'

It is also a kind of team picture, and Ford has always worked well when given another character against whom he has the freedom to play. He got on particularly well with Gene Wilder, whose manic on-screen performances relaxed his reticent personality. Ford has always found it difficult to let himself go. Part of the reason he feels so drawn towards acting is that it allows him certain means and methods of expression through the playing of other characters. At this time, though he was building a reputation as a committed actor who always remained professional, he was also becoming known for a certain on-set aloofness. His involvement with Wilder, however, went some way towards rectifying that.

It is interesting to hear him stress to what extent he enjoyed working with Robert Aldrich. Every time Ford takes part in a picture he finds particularly fulfilling, it is always the relationship with his director that he mentions. He sees acting as a co-operative effort, and has never taken kindly to being instructed by an inflexible director. That may be why he found working on *Hanover Street* with Peter Hyams so disappointing: Hyams' vision of the film contrasted so markedly with Ford's that there was no possibility of compromise. And compromise, understanding, and sheer professionalism have always been the watchwords of the man from Chicago.

Hanover Street and *The Frisco Kid* could not have been more different: one was a traditional romance; the other a tale of male camaraderie. Ford had performed capably in both. He was learning to hold his own in the company of other, more experienced and certainly better known actors, and to turn his hand to a variety of roles.

The last two years had been hectic with four feature films following closely on the heels of *Star Wars*. None of them had really given Ford the freedom from cliché and typecasting that he sought, but now at least people took him seriously. And the 'big bucks' were just around the corner once again.

5

A Perfect State of Hibernation

By 1979 Harrison Ford's relationship with Melissa Matheson was developing and the happiness he now experienced in his personal life seemed to dampen his enthusiasm for acting. His interest in carpentry continued even as his film projects became increasingly successful, and for the time being he was content to immerse himself in his woodwork. He had earned enough money over the past six years to feel no financial pressures, and he had no desire to prove himself the greatest living actor. His cinematic career was put on 'hold'.

In 1978 George Lucas had approached Ford to repeat his role in *American Graffiti* for the less than imaginatively titled *More American Graffiti*. This time there was a neat little twist to the characters: for the follow-up, Ford would be *Officer* Falfa, a narcotics cop who was less a pillar of the establishment than its rotten, if jingoistic core. It was a nice idea, but Ford was not impressed. He respectfully declined, giving as his reason the fact that he had no wish to go back to playing cameo roles after spending such a tortuous apprenticeship making a success of his career. The truth may have been a combination of that and the effects of his relationship with Melissa Matheson; or even that, with *Apocalypse Now* due to come out in the same year, he did not want to be associated with another Vietnam movie. But for whatever reasons, it led to a wise choice: *More American Graffiti* proved a major failure, taking two years to break even after release.

Ford remained in fairly close contact with George Lucas, however. He had, in fact, not been out of touch since the initial meeting on *American Graffiti*, and the director felt that it would be worthwhile to work together again. The failure of *More American Graffiti* quickly nullified the adulation Lucas had received after *Star Wars* – at least on the part of the film financiers and accountants – and the pressure that put upon him could only to be dissipated by the success of his next project. This was also a film which was to be of significant though not cataclysmic importance to Harrison Ford's career. In late 1978 the director contacted the actor once again, this time to detail his ideas for the second part of the current *Star Wars* trilogy, a film entitled *The Empire Strikes Back*. The bad guys were to make a come-back.

It would be fair to say that Ford was less than intrigued by the prospect: unlike the other principal players, he was only contracted to a one-picture deal, and had more freedom to refuse Lucas' approaches. Having at one stage decided to stop being Han Solo on-screen, he had no great urge now to make what he now saw as a backwards career move. However, gentleman that he was, he was soon enamoured of, if not infected by Lucas' enthusiasm, and signed up for the film. There was one proviso – that his part should be expanded.

Along with the other actors, he was offered further profit participation, though Lucas, canny as always, also gave them an option to sell the percentage back for a flat fee. It was a package Ford could not refuse.

Lucas was relieved; to date, too many things had gone wrong. Typically, even the preliminary evolution of Empire had met with more than its fair share of obstacles. The story for the film had risen out of Lucas' original concept for Star Wars, but this time, rather than write the screenplay himself, he decided he would provide a basic scene and dialogue outline and hire someone else to shape it into something more substantial. After some deliberation, he chose the established and gifted screen-writer Leigh Brackett. Unfortunately, Brackett died after completing the first draft, and, once again Lucas had to look elsewhere for a writer.

It did not take him long to decide upon Lawrence Kasdan who, although fairly new to screen-writing, had just completed the script for *Raiders of the Lost Ark*, also for him. Lucas had, in fact, offered Kasdan the job before looking at the *Raiders* script, albeit though with the proviso, 'Of course, if I hate *Raiders* I'll take back this offer'. Kasdan was pleased to accept. He was provided with Lucas' second draft from Brackett's original, and he knew immediately the course he had to chart. 'I felt that my responsibility was to understand the *Star Wars* galaxy, *not* the basic concepts of science fiction,' he told *Starlog* magazine. 'Star Wars doesn't have all that much to do with SF or what its fans are interested in. . . From what I've read, a lot of science fiiction seems to be based on extensions of real life in a way that the *Star Wars* series doesn't really care about. . . On *Empire*, we were all working within George's grand scheme.'

Once again, Lucas was pulling around him a particular group of people, creating an ensemble whose talent and commitment to the project would shine through on-screen. If anything, it was this approach, this almost anti-Hollywood attitude, that convinced Ford to join in despite his reservations. Almost despite himself, he had become part of a team that would be associated with nearly all of the most profitable films of the next decade.

The most immediate problem now facing Lucas was one of expectation. It had been estimated that, in the three months since its release, *Star Wars* had played to more people more quickly than any other film in the history of cinema. It had taken over $100 million in rentals in that period alone, and had made George Lucas a very wealthy man. There was a lot to live up to. *Star Wars* had proved such a resounding success primarily because its invention was intensified by its sheer novelty. Quite simply, nobody had ever done it before. With *The Empire Strikes Back*, that novelty value had to be replaced by something more substantial. The whole world was waiting.

Lucas knew that, and he wasted no time. Once he had his stars and his writer, he went looking for a director. It was perhaps the most fundamental casting job of all. Lucas would effectively be handing over the reins to another and, although he would ensure he retained final control, what went up on the screen would be someone else's interpretation of the adventure. Lucas also needed someone capable of dealing with the less than enthusiastic attitude of his performers – primarily Harrison Ford. He had already decided to leave the fate of Han Solo unresolved because he could not be sure that Ford would return for the final instalment of the trilogy; he needed a director with a firm but unobtrusive hand. If this film failed, so did the whole *Star Wars* corpus. There was no room for mistakes.

After some months considering anyone and everyone – even Steven Spielberg was approached at one stage, but he was busy elsewhere – Lucas eventually chose Irving Kershner. Kershner had been a lecturer and researcher at USCLA at the time Lucas had attended the college – it is curious how everyone associated with Lucas' successes seemed to share his past – and had proved himself an able and efficient director. His last film had been John Carpenter's

The Eyes of Laura Mars, and he had proved himself able to bring in a project on time with as few problems as possible. They were qualities which would be sorely needed on the shooting schedule of *Empire*. Unfortunately, from Lucas' point of view they were also to be found wanting.

The film was to be shot in three different locations: the glacial landscape of Norway, which would represent the ice-planet of Hoth; the increasingly used Elstree studios near London; and Lucas' own Industrial Light and Magic workshops in Marin County, California. Travelling between the three was not going to be the easiest of tasks to perform.

Harrison Ford was particularly inconvenienced by the travel schedule. His previous experience of being dragged away from home for interminable periods had been a primary cause of the breakdown of his marriage, and he had no wish to go through that sort of emotional upheaval again. As usual, however, Lucas was particularly deft in convincing him of the relatively undemanding nature of the project, and eventually Ford believed him. Indeed, on the shooting schedule delivered to him the instructions seemed simple enough: to arrive at Finse in Norway on 6 March 1979 for filming. As always, however, things proved a little more complicated in practice. After flying from London to Oslo, Ford took a train to the film location. Unfortunately, it did not quite get him there. At the ski resort of Geilo, the Scandinavian winter closed in once and for all, stranding him in almost arctic conditions. From there, Ford took two taxis, and then rode shotgun on a snowplough, before finally reaching his destination. 'What a way to run a railway!' he is reported to have said.

Ford never seemed to find anything to do with his career easy, but the fact that this incident appeared not to ruffle him in the slightest – seemed, in fact, to appeal to him and renew his appetite for the project – indicates his resilience and liking for a challenge. The more hurdles that were put in his way, the more Harrison Ford chose to jump them.

Before *Empire* had been set in motion, George Lucas, Irving Kirshner and Lawrence Kasdan had discussed the film to death; everything had been considered, reconsidered and finally codified, with no room for change. Then along came Ford, who was in the habit of offering unexpected if appropriate advice whenever a scene seemed in danger of lacking direction. In the company of Kirshner, he began to crack the tablets, much to the displeasure of Lucas and his writer.

Perhaps the most important, and contentious, of Ford's contributions came in the scene where Solo is about to be immersed in the carbon-freeze and the Princess tells him she loves him. According to the script, Solo had no lines to speak, but that gave the impression that the character knew just what fate the villain Darth Vader had in store for him. Reacting against this, Ford suggested everything from the clothes he should wear in the scene, to Leia's expression of love and his prosaic answer, 'I know'. It brought about a complete reorientation of the dramatic stresses in the scene, and the fact that Ford was able to convince not only the director but also his fellow actors of the merit of the changes indicates the degree of respect he inspired in others. No one takes direction, especially by a co-star, lightly.

Carrie Fisher in particular found Ford's suggestions invaluable, and always well-considered. Her role in the scene became that much more carefully defined because Ford had taken time to understand the precise needs and motivations of the character of Solo at that time. Not everyone was pleased with the way things transpired, however. Lawrence Kasdan's observations about the relationship between the characters revealed a lot about the extent of Ford's influence, as well Kasdan's reservations: 'Han and Leia's relationship is not at all what I envisioned,' he told *Starlog* magazine. 'I could be the only one who feels this way, but I thought that their romance had a touch of falseness about it. Han and Leia's scenes were among what I was proudest of in my script, but they barely remained. Their being changed had a lot to do with the circumstances of filming, Kershner and the actors' feelings about doing their roles again. . . I wasn't crazy about Harrison Ford in *Empire*.' He reputedly told Lucas: 'That's not the way I wrote it, George.'

Kasdan's comments indicate the extent to which Ford did adapt and extend whatever part he was playing. He may have done this to a greater extent on *Empire* simply because he was reprising a role. Without any new ideas to bring to the character, he probably felt that Han Solo would not have developed sufficiently to keep the part interesting and demanding – both for him, and for the audience.

The character of Han Solo was not the only aspect of the film that did not develop as planned; from Lucas' point of view the making of *The Empire Strikes Back* proved a disaster from start to finish. Apart from the fact that the daily rushes he saw bore no relation to the film he had originally envisioned, he encountered severe financial problems. The original budget had been set at $15 million. It had risen to $18.5 million even before the cameras started rolling. By the time things got underway, it was $22 million and rising, finally reaching a peak of $28 million. This was a terrifyingly expensive project, even in Hollywood terms, and Lucas had his shirt riding on it. To obtain the necessary financial backing for the production simply to continue, he was forced to pledge much of what he had earned from *Graffiti* and *Star Wars*. And that inevitably caused problems.

The intense pressures of the situation inevitably communicated themselves to all concerned, but Lucas' insight in casting a trio of central characters who could work perfectly together under all conditions kept the acting side under control. He really had picked an excellent team. As Ford told Alan Arnold: 'It is very hard for me to look objectively at the film. It's George's creation. He gave himself a beautiful princess in Leia and a callow youth in Luke. He gave himself a sage warrior in Ben Kenobi, and he gave himself a character called Han Solo, who is described as "a cynical space pirate". But he's not really a cynic, and the phrase "space pirate" doesn't really indicate what he does. In fact, what he does in the story is to function as a kind of synthesizer. He's the most realistic character and consequently, in a way, the easiest one to play. It is a pleasure to play that kind of part. When I read the script I knew nothing about science fiction. I read the script and asked myself "can they really make a movie out of this?" I had no idea how it would feel creating Han. What I did understand was the relation among the four characters I have mentioned. . . Han helps make everything contemporary, recognizably human, in a way. Anyway, it worked for a lot of people. I was just part of the equation George dreamed up.'

For Ford generally, therefore, it was a success despite his doubts about taking the part. He enjoyed working with his fellow actors and Irving Kirshner, of whom he observed: 'He's a different kind of director. We had a very close relationship on the level of freedom to contribute'. He was also ultimately happy with his performance. There is a change of emphasis in Solo's character from *Star Wars* to *Empire*: Solo becomes more convincing, more obviously flawed; and this time he lacks the irritating storybook virtues which grated in the first film.

The success of Solo's metamorphosis was partly due to Lucas and Kasdan's collaboration on the screenplay, and to their realization that the characters had to be shown to learn from their experiences, *Empire* could too easily have become a re-run of the predecessor. More than that, it was a sign of Harrison Ford's rapidly developing skill and confidence on-screen, and his performance amply justified George Lucas' expressed confidence in him: 'I liked Harrison from working on *Graffiti*,' he told Alan Arnold. 'I thought he was a very talented actor, and I enjoyed working with him. But when I considered him for the *Star Wars* trilogy, I was afraid I was being influenced by the fact that I liked him, that I was familiar with his work, that I was thinking of him for the part because of my previous associations with him. So I did tests with lots of others, too. But I just couldn't find anybody who had his qualities as an actor and fit my concept of the character as well as he did.'

It had taken three films, but finally Ford and Lucas had developed an almost symbiotic relationship, in which both had the freedom to experiment and extend their respective talents. It was a relationship from which they would find encouragement and confidence – and not a little material advantage. Ford, Lucas and soon Steven Spielberg eventually developed a professional relationship so interlinked that it became almost like a benevolent Cosa Nostra of the film world; they created a private gentleman's club where an interest in blockbuster features was the price of admission. Almost despite himself, Lucas was beginning to use actors he had nurtured and seen prove themselves under his wing, taking an almost fatherly pride in their success. Of them all, Harrison Ford is perhaps the most famous, though Richard Dreyfuss, Robert Duvall and Ron Howard have all been part of the Lucasfilm empire.

Empire was not so much a film, therefore, as a catalyst. It served to forge relationships and build abilities. It was also instrumental in crystallizing Lucas' own vision of *Star Wars*: for the first time he allowed others to show him his creation through *their* eyes. Ford's portrayal of Han Solo brought the character to life in a way that Lucas found remarkable; an incidental character had become one of the most popular individuals in modern film. And the understated manner in which Ford played the part served as a perfect foil to the special effects, carnival, and heroic performances of the other characters. Everyone seemed happy enough.

The film was not perfect, however. The sheer pace and adventure that would be seen in *Raiders of the Lost Ark* could be perceived somewhere behind the smoke and clamour of battle on-screen, but it was more immediately violent than *Star Wars*, as if there was a coarse, physical quality that Lucas wanted to get across (this may have been Kasdan's influence, though the tale may also have lost a little in the telling). Unfortunately, there seemed a certain gratuitousness behind the violence that swung the film away from its idealistic origins. This is exemplified in the scene where Luke has his hand sliced off by Vader, whilst the fact that he has a replacement fitted so quickly and easily lends a disturbing quality to the action. Lucas had a credible enough dramatic reason for the amputation scene – that Luke is in danger of becoming as much machinery and silicon chips as Vader is already – but it was somehow badly done. The thin line between reality and fantasy, so carefully trod in *Star Wars*, now seemed a little smudged and indistinct.

There have been frequent criticisms of Lucas' films, often from the very people who envy him his success. Many say that they are really nothing more than celluloid comic books, all special effects and big bangs. This is an accusation that causes Ford to spring quickly to Lucas' defence: 'In America we have evolved a film style which is perhaps different to that in Europe,' he once observed to Alan McKenzie, 'And I feel that there is as much opportunity for expression and action in a scene without dialogue as there is in a scene with. So I don't see that similarity with comic books. Because it's not literature doesn't mean it's a comic book for me. And that's the extension that's being made. . . I've heard this said a number of times, that the characters are less real than they might be in other circumstances. . . I think it's very wrong to look down our noses at "entertainment".'

The fact that Lucas ended the film in such an indeterminate manner, with Solo possibly dead from the carbon-freezing process, also brought forth a lot of criticism. In truth, it represented a combination of Lucas' brave, all-or-nothing approach to the production – it was the second film in the trilogy and there was more to come – and of his realization that he could not afford to make any of his actors feel they were indispensable, particularly Harrison Ford. As Mark Hamill told Alan Arnold: 'Look at what's happening to Harrison. He wasn't at all sure whether he wanted to repeat his role as Solo, and he's not at all committed to doing it a third time. So George has left him in limbo in this one. As Lando Calrissian says after Han is hauled up from the carbo-freezing chamber: "He's in a perfect state of hibernation". So George has given himself the option. Han is not vital to future stories. It's up to Harrison, I guess, as to whether Han comes back into the saga.'

Ford took a slightly different view of the situation. However doubtful he might have been about playing the part initially, it was *his* part, and he did not like any talk of it being taken away from him. 'The cliff-hanger is because the trilogy was really constructed in the classic form of a three-act play,' he said: 'Naturally, there are going to be questions in the second act which have to be resolved in the third. I guess it really depends on what you go to a movie for. I figure there was at least eleven dollars worth of entertainment in "Empire". So if you paid four bucks and didn't get an ending, you're still seven dollars ahead of the game.' Spoken in the true spirit of Han Solo.

With hindsight, it is Ford's perception of the film that carries more weight than that expressed by Hamill. Lucas had planned the basic plot of the *Star Wars* trilogy years before, and the expediencey of putting Solo in hibernation of some sort was always a likely, if not a definite option. And it has to be said the ploy worked: the debate as to whether Solo would be brought back to life raged right up until the release of the third film in the trilogy. Members of Lucas' entourage swore on pain of death to reveal nothing of Solo's fate, and the secret survived until the opening night of the *Return of the Jedi*. As in the old Republic studio's serials of the thirties and forties, the audience was left on the edge of their seats in anticipation. This time, they had to wait a little longer than a week for the answer.

The Empire Strikes Back was released on 21 May 1980, and *Star Wars* fans were queueing round the block for over three days beforehand. There was an increasing sense of desperate anticipation; this was worse than the World Series and the

Superbowl combined. For may of them *Empire* was more than just another film, it was an integral part of their lives. Lucas' creation had struck a common nerve in a way that no other film had ever managed to do. It took only three months for him to recoup all his money – over $30 million – and the film went on to reap over $500 million dollars around the world. It proved to be the third most popular film ever – after its predecessor and *E.T.* – and was hailed everywhere as the perfect sequel to *Star Wars*.

Its success also significantly affected Ford's life style. His profit percentage, now over two per cent, came in more than useful. He still receives regular royalty cheques as the film continues to earn. Less tangibly, but perhaps more importantly, with *Empire* he seemed to develop a new, less flippant attitude towards the power of film – and it showed. His performance reveals a marked improvement, both in the way he presents himself to the camera, and also in the way he conveys a greater range of meaning with less effort than before.

The film was thus a turning point in Ford's attitude to acting, as well as his career. He became less disdainful and earnest, more open and receptive to the whole filming process. Lucas' fascination for the concept of cinema, for its possibilities, and its power literally to liberate something within the individual, may not have been taken wholly on board by Ford, but something certainly rubbed off. Paradoxically he learned more from this repetition of a role than he had from his previous five projects. 'I see my films as *films*,' he observed at the time. 'I see the characters as expressive, as full as the film has time. I don't see any limitation on what a film can do. And as long as I can contribute something different and valuable to it, that's enough for me.' All this from a man who wandered into film because he flunked college.

The Empire Strikes Back revitalized Ford's reputation as an actor of talent and subtlety, and he looked for more demanding roles to come his way. Little could he realize that his next project would catapult him into the realms of superstardom, or that it would be another George Lucas brainchild.

6

The Great Adventure

'I don't want to be a movie star,' observed Harrison Ford, 'I want to be in movies that are stars.'

He seemed almost to kick back against the peculiar kind of stardom that had so quickly been forced upon him. For many people he was not simply associated with the character, he actually was Han Solo. Lucas' sequence of films had somehow gone beyond simply presenting fantasy characters on-screen; they had portrayed a world which had become real to literally millions of people. For Harrison Ford in particular that caused a few problems. It is bad enough being the object of hero worship as yourself, but when you are exalted in your fictional persona, it can be a little tough to handle. He explained his attitude to Jane Goodwin: 'I was fortunate to get Han Solo, which pleased me because I liked his sense of humour. I had no expectation of the level of adulation the film would bring. I had no ambition for such star status. I just wanted to make a living as an actor, and I never even fantasized about the kind of prestige I have now.'

For over fifteen years, it seemed that Ford had deliberately chosen the less spectacular films that were offered him precisely because he knew they would reduce his public profile. Then, following *Star Wars*, stardom had been thrust upon him, and had instigated in him a reaction of sorts against his success. He needed time to find out exactly what it was he wanted from the cinema. Yet every sojourn out in the relative

75

wilderness of efficient but unexceptional films such as *Heroes* and *The Frisco Kid* seemed destined to end with him returning to his old friend and mentor, George Lucas, who was perhaps the one man to whom he was prepared to trust his acting career. This is ironic because Lucas was in part the cause of the problem, but in his flair for success Ford saw the possibility of escaping from the millstone that Solo threatened to become.

Lucas had come up with an idea for an 'A-quality, B-movie based on grade Z 1930s serials', a little adventure to be called *Raiders of the Lost Ark*. As with all things with which the director was involved, however, there would be a long and involved period of gestation before anything tangible was seen. He had first had the idea for the film back in 1975 whilst he was working on the script for *Star Wars*. A confirmed addict of the old Republic studio's cliff-hanger serials of the thirties, Lucas wanted to create a hero who represented all heroes – from the enigmatic Zorro to the rough diamond Fred C. Dobbs in *Treasure of the Sierra Madre*. The bullwhip used at moments of high drama by Indiana Jones was taken from the character of Zorro, champion of the weak and oppressed, and that was the type of legendary, if somewhat unreal heroism to which Lucas addressed himself. Jones was to be a remarkable individual, a gifted but mysterious loner, who always knew just who the good guys were. He was also to be a character modelled in part on Lucas' own personality, but whereas Luke Skywalker was the kind of screwed-up adolescent he had actually been, Indiana Jones was the strong, independent, 'never-lose-your-hat-in-a-fight' kind of hero he had always imagined himself to be. The kind who always got the girl in High School.

Even whilst he was involved in *Star Wars*, Lucas mapped

out three or four possible story outlines for his new adventure film but had to put them to one side in order to hammer out a production deal for the film in hand. Some months later, he met up with an old colleague, director Philip Kaufman, and over dinner told him about his plans. Kaufman suggested incorporating the idea of the Ark of the Covenant, a desperate search against time, and the wicked force of Hitler's minions into the story. Short of an animal co-star, this film was going to have everything. Lucas liked the idea immediately. He was astute enough to realize that by incorporating all those elements into his story he could not fail to strike some kind of chord in almost every cinema-goer. It also suited his penchant for editing together numerous different story elements into a cohesive, energetic whole.

For some time it looked as if the two men would collaborate on the project, but then Kaufman took on another film and those plans were shelved. Lucas turned his attention back to *Star Wars* and the rest, as they say, is history.

The character of Indiana Smith, which was Lucas' first choice of name for his hero, refused to lie down and play possum. According to legend, when Lucas disappeared to an Hawaiian beach in 1977 to avoid what he was sure would be a disastrous opening for *Star Wars*, he was quickly followed by Steven Spielberg with news of just how wrong he had been. Whilst the two men sat building a sand castle in a ninety-degree heat, Lucas chatted about his ideas for a hero who belonged back in the old school. Spielberg was immediately convinced that this was a terrific idea, and he saw it as the perfect opportunity to pay a special kind of homage to his formative years.

Though Spielberg was enamoured of film in a different way to Lucas – he had not gone to film school, in fact his film career began when, at the age of nineteen he bought himself a briefcase, strolled past the security guard at Universal Studios and never went home – he similarly believed in the power of film as *entertainment*. Anything else had to spring from that primary assumption, and because the two men had much the same ideas and points of view about films the collaboration was embarked upon.

Spielberg brought a new insight into the way the film should be approached, one which would prove influential in the choice of Harrison Ford as leading man. He suggested that Lucas' original idea of a playboy adventurer should be toned down, and that the film should stress the physicality of the character more, emphasizing the ambivalence of personality which made him more interesting. It was Ford, later, who provided the most succinct description of that approach: 'Indiana Jones is an archaeologist. In his spare time he's a grave-robber.'

Lucas saw the character from a different perspective. 'Indy can do anything,' he observed. 'He's a college professor and he's got his Cary Grant side, too.' And, as he observed to Dale Pollock, he knew precisely the kind of actor that was needed: 'He has to be a person we can look up to. We're doing a role model for kids, so we have to be careful. We need someone who's honest and true and trusting.' The way Lucas described him, Indiana Jones was going to have to be a cross between Superman and Abraham Lincoln. This is significant because it indicates how seriously he took his responsibilities as a film-maker. He was perfectly aware of the influence his work would exercise over those who saw it, especially over the large numbers of adolescents and children who made up a significant slice of the Lucasfilm audience.

Before he could turn his attention towards casting,

however, there were various preliminaries that had to be addressed. He did not yet know who was going to write it. Towards the end of 1977, Steven Spielberg sent Lucas a script called *Continental Divide*, written by Californian advertising copywriter Lawrence Kasdan, an absolute beginner as far as Hollywood was concerned. The director, perhaps because the thought of giving such a big break to a gifted newcomer appealed to him, decided to take things further. As Kasdan explained to *Starlog* magazine: 'Steven was the producer at Universal originally connected with that company's interest in *Continental Divide*, before they won the bidding for my script. When he first read it, he told my agent "I'm going to make an adventure movie with George Lucas and I think that Larry would be a good person to write it". That film turned out to be *Raiders of the Lost Ark*. He asked my agent if he could show *Continental Divide* to George . . . who fortunately liked it quite a bit. The two of them then invited me to a meeting with themselves and Frank Marshall, the film's producer. That conference was when we made the deal for me to write *Raiders*, which made me very happy.'

For some months the four men sat down and hammered out their ideas for the film. Lucas' approach was typically direct: breaking the plot down into seperate incidents, each with its own action and climax. Kasdan was more reserved and deliberate in his approach, perhaps looking for more depth and subtlety in the characters than Lucas thought necessary. It proved to be a time of intense invention. The conferences were always heated, though never antagonistic, and eventually compromise was reached on all the important points. From then on, it took Kasdan approximately six months to write the script and flesh out the various ideas. 'It took that long because writing *Raiders* was a big job,' he remembered. 'Our outlining was immense but not detailed. We knew who the three main characters would be, but there wasn't a word in anybody's mouth. There were no broad-strokes and real structure to the plot of *Raiders*. I had to come up with all of that.'

Part of the reason he had to 'come up with all of that' was because Lucas' emphasis on action and 'thrills and spills' meant he often overlooked the simple necessities of motive and character development. With Kasdan on board it became less of an immediate problem, but later on his and to a lesser extent Spielberg's lack of attention to detail would catch up with them.

Kasdan carried out a great deal of in-depth research in order to get the period detail just right, ensuring he did not make any glaring mistakes about archaeology or the his-toricity of the Third Reich. Between initiation and com-pletion, the script underwent five separate metamorphoses. It was to be changed even further during filming, in response to the development of the character of Indiana Jones and the ideas Harrison Ford brought to bear. Once Kasdan had fin-ished his task, it was time for Lucas and Spielberg to find someone to bring the hero to life.

Both men realized that they needed an actor with a par-ticular blend of physical presence and careful insouciance to play the part. After much consultation, their first choice was Tom Selleck, who had just completed the pilot for the *Magnum PI* series. They approached CBS with the suggestion that the series be held off for a year because their star was bound to be much more famous after the film's release. No deal, said the mighty television company with a lack of fore-sight that must still rankle. Ironically, Selleck could have taken the part after all, for an actors' strike delayed the shooting of the *Magnum* series. *'Raiders* was able to keep going in Europe because of a special dispensation,' remembered Selleck, 'But we couldn't make a move on Hawaii. So, in fact, I could probably have done both. . . I felt entitled to get something out of it, though, and kept telling people, "That was my part, you know".' To his great credit, he exhibited no bitterness over Ford's success: 'It's hard to imagine anyone being better than Harrison Ford in it. He was quite wonderful. It really was his film.'

Had Selleck taken the part, Lucas' original concept of the playboy adventurer might have come much more forcefully to the fore. The film might also have lacked a certain power. Selleck has perhaps a greater sense of comedy than Harrison Ford, but his on-screen heroics lack the credibility Ford brings to his acting. And the friendly romantic relationship between the central characters Jones and Marion Ravenwood might have been less equal under the influence of Thomas Magnum's macho suavity. Indiana Jones PI just does not seem to work.

At the time of CBS' refusal, Lucas and Spielberg were faced with a serious problem: once their first choice was deemed unavailable, they realized they had no real contingency plans about hiring a replacement. 'We were looking for a leading man over six months,' recalled Spielberg. 'We wanted an unknown originally – a total unknown. Conceitedly, George and I wanted to make a star of Johnny the construction worker from Malibu. We couldn't find a construction worker in Malibu, so we began to look at more substantial people in the film industry.

'We were stuck, we had three weeks left to cast the part of Indiana Jones, and there was nobody close. Then I saw *The Empire Strikes Back*, and I said Harrison Ford *is* Indiana Jones. I called George Lucas and said, "He's right under our noses". George said, "I know who you're going to say." I said, "Who?" and he said, "Harrison Ford." "Right." "let's get him," he said. And we did.' The immediacy with which Lucas acquiesced indicates that in the back of his mind he had always felt that Ford was perfect for the part. In interviews since the film's release, he has sometimes intimated that after their work together on the *Star Wars* films he was inclined to choose Ford for the part.

Later on, with typical diplomacy, Spielberg embroidered the story of hiring Ford, and omitted the part about offering the role to Selleck altogether. 'Harrison Ford was the only person George and I saw playing Indiana Jones,' he said. 'He is a remarkable combination of Errol Flynn from *The Adventures of Don Juan* and Humphrey Bogart as Fred C. Dobbs in *Treasure of the Sierra Madre*. He can be villainous and romantic all at once.'

It sounded like the perfect role for Ford to play. It would make significantly greater demands upon him than the parts of Han Solo or Bob Falfa, and was yet the kind of larger-than-life figure he enjoyed playing. It also offered him the chance to take the lead. He was not immediately convinced by the part however. He had been aware of the script for some time – had in fact seen Kasdan's screenplay almost as soon as Lucas – but he evidently felt no urge to put himself forward. 'They knew where I was,' he commented. Once the offer had been made, however, Ford showed no hesitation in accepting. He did express one reservation about the role: 'I was a little concerned that Indiana Jones was reminiscent of Han Solo when I read the script. I didn't want to keep reprising the same role, so Steven and I made use of the opportunities in Lawrence Kasdan's screenplay to put a little space between the characters. We talked it over on the 'plane to London, going through the script for over ten hours. By the time we landed, we knew exactly where it was going.'

Ford was perfectly aware that, with a little work, the part offered a lot more scope for personal input than his previous roles had, and in *Skywalkin'* he notes that, 'It was clearly the most dominant single character in any of George's films, quite in variance with his theories about movie stars and what they mean.

He clearly recognized the intrinsic power and charisma of the character, 'The great thing about Indiana Jones,' he explained to James H. Burns, 'is that he's a far more complex character than any other hero I've played. He isn't a competitive hero like characters played by Errol Flynn or Douglas Fairbanks. He survives by his wits. There's no space hardware around to help him – often only his two fists. But he's a survivor, and although he gets hurt a lot, he wins through in the end.'

Despite his initial reservations, it was apparent that the part of Indiana Jones greatly appealed to Ford. He can have had no idea of the overwhelming success that was to follow, but the idea of 'a simple story told quick and fast' with such a dominant central character offered a way out of the stagnation that his career had entered into. As he made clear, however, it was only the involvement of people whose abilities he trusted that finally convinced him to say yes. 'George had called me and said he would like me to do Steven Spielberg's next film if Steven and I got along,' he told journalist Derek Taylor. 'I had met Steven once, casually. And George told me right away that there would be three of these films, but only if the first film was successful.

'I was convinced enough of the talent of the people

involved to believe that the first one was going to be a good film. That is the most important thing. And one of the circumstances we haven't really spoken about is that I hadn't been able to find a project I liked in the three months before.'

So Lucas and Spielberg got their man, and, as the results would show, it was surprising that they ever considered anyone else for the part. Ford revelled in the challenge presented to him, spending a great deal of time looking for ways he might extend the character and bring his own perceptions to bear.

Faced with such commitment, the two directors knew how important it was to put together a quality supporting cast, a group of actors and actresses who could provide the level of ensemble playing required to complement the exploits of a college-professor-cum-adventurer. For the female lead, Spielberg 'auditioned' various candidates in a kitchen at Lucasfilm in Los Angeles. Between the soft drinks and idle chatter, the director looked for a woman capable of perfectly reflecting the character of Marion Ravenwood, who is in many ways a mirror-image of Indiana Jones. 'Karen Allen was the most professional actress to come into our readings,' remembered Spielberg. 'She was polished and she came prepared. After that, we just kept saying, "not as good as Karen".'

It proved to be the perfect choice, and the actress herself remembers how she felt an immediate empathy with the role. 'From the beginning I knew pretty quickly that I would work well with Steven,' she told Derek Taylor,' because the screen tests took two or three hours, I guess. Each of them. And just in the course of doing the tests we really got somewhere, putting our heads together with the character, finding ways to put added dimensions into it, which was wonderful.'

Harrison Ford had his leading lady. To fill in the all-important gaps, Spielberg went further afield, selecting such able and gifted actors as Ronald Lacey, John Rhys-Davies and Paul Freeman. Ford was pleased with the way things were going. Typically, however, he attempted to play down his forthcoming involvement: 'The directors and the writers are the real poets of the system. The job of the actor is just to tell the story. . .' he said at the time.

But what a story. Now that most of the preliminary work had been done, Geoege Lucas began to hand over the reins to Steven Spielberg – as far as he was ever able to hand them over where an idea of his own was concerned. Although on paper they each had their own tasks to contend with, the triumvirate of Ford, Spielberg and Lucas were to work closely together in bringing Indiana Jones to life. It would be a long adventure.

The locations had already been scouted and studio time booked, and Ford prepared himself for some of the most demanding 'physical acting' he had ever had to perform. Talk was cheap, ahead lay a gruellingly active seventy-three days, during which the battered trilby would become almost permanently fixed to his head, and he would prove himself proficient with the bullwhip that was to be Indy's trademark. 'The only reason I learnt to use it was so's I didn't whip my own head off,' he remembered.

On 23 June 1980, three years and one month after George Lucas had first mentioned the idea to Steven Spielberg, the cast and crew of *Raiders of the Lost Ark* arrived at La Rochelle, France for principal shooting. Spielberg had arranged for a copy of a World War Two German U-boat to be sent over from Bavaria where it had been built for use on a film called *Das Boot*. He had realized it was perfect for the scene where Indy has to swim from the tramp steamer the *Bantu Wind* to the Nazi submarine, and Harrison Ford soon discovered that his introduction to his character was to be rough and ready. Spielberg wanted Jones to 'come away cut and bruised and battered and wonderfully in pain', though he had perhaps not informed Ford, who had to swim through rough sea himself. It was an experience few stuntmen would have relished, but he maintained: 'Swimming to the submarine didn't involve danger, it only involved discomfort.'

The shooting in France was completed swiftly and efficiently on schedule – with fifteen minutes to spare. The company were elated that such a potentially difficult shoot – sea filming is notoriously unpredictable – had gone so well. 'The first two days the weather was very rough,' Robert Watts, assistant producer, told the *Collector*'s magazine. 'Thursday got very rough. We managed to stay out, even though a lot of people got seasick.'

On 30 June the cast and crew transferred to Elstree Studios. For Harrison Ford, always the professional, that meant another opportunity to enjoy a particularly favourite luxury: 'I like English beer,' he observed. 'That's just one good reason I like coming to England.' It was a good job that he felt fortified by the local brew: the work at Elstree was to be demanding even for an actor of his stamina and physique.

For three months before the crew arrived, five of the studio's sound stages had been taken over for the building of two major sets – the immense structures of the Well of the Souls and the Temple of the Chachapoyan Warriors. Spielberg required full-size versions of all the scenes envisaged by George Lucas, and that was not all. For the scene where Indy finally discovered the Ark he ordered over 6,000 snakes of all shapes and sizes – from cobras, pythons and boa constrictors to thousands of harmless but no more endearing reptiles. And all of them *always* moved in the direction least expected of them.

Harrison Ford proved serenely unperturbed by the snakes; as a youngster he had worked at a boy scout camp as a counsellor, and had revelled in collecting snakes and identifying them. But for his co-stars things initially proved a little difficult. 'I've never really been around snakes very much,' recalled Karen Allen. 'I've grown fond of them, except the pythons, the ones that bite – I'm not fond of those. It feels a little odd being so physically unprotected in all of those scenes. It works well for me and, at the same time, it makes it worse. Harrison has his boots and gloves, and leather clothes, and I have naked arms, and nothing on my legs, and bare feet. In the beginning that was tougher than it is now because I just couldn't stand the snakes on my feet. But I've gotten used to them. Now I have to keep reminding myself that they're snakes.'

Things did not go exactly as planned, however. The script called for the snakes to be afraid of fire, but unfortunately snakes cannot read. Being cold-blooded they move towards the heat, which meant that the actors would suddenly find themselves ankle-deep in reptiles. Spielberg tried to be comforting about the whole affair, but only succeeded in revealing just how chaotic and dangerous the scene must have appeared to those taking part. 'The pythons aren't poisonous,' he told *Starlog* magazine, 'but they do bite. . . And when they bite they don't let go. The cobras came from India, as did the anti-toxin serum. The serum was out-dated by a year, so we couldn't shoot the cobras until we had the fresh serum. Then another shipment came in from Paris and *that* was out-dated. Just before I would have gone over schedule on the Well of Souls set, fresh serum showed up. We were able to shoot the whole sequence with the cobras in two days.'

It was becoming increasingly apparent that *Raiders of the Lost Ark* was the most idiosyncratic of Harrison Ford's films so far, and it was not just the snakes that were causing problems. Spielberg had decided to opt for a particularly stylized type of presentation, a celluloid version of the comic book adventures of the thirties and forties, and that meant a shift in approach for everyone involved. As Spielberg so succinctly put it: 'We're now moving out of the Al Pacino school of drama into the Sam Peckinpah school of action.'

The development of the screenplay meant that Ford's character was involved in some ninety per cent of that action, and he chose to do as much of it himself as was possible. 'Harrison is physical to a fault,' Spielberg remembered. 'He does most of his own stunt work throughout the movie. It's really him doing some of the most incredible things. He was always in there prepared to do a stunt. There are four or five very risky scenes that Terry Leonard, J.R. Randall and Vic Armstrong did for him. J.R. Randall was our stunt gaffer, and he wouldn't let Harrison do any stunts that were potentially fatal. But Harrison did most everything else. Anything that simply promised serious injury or total disability, Harrison did; anything that promised death through fatal miscalculation, Terry, Vic and J.R. did. And everybody survived. That's the most amazing thing about the *Raiders* saga – everybody survived.'

There were various reasons why Ford decided to be so deeply involved in what most actors would consider a less than enticing aspect of the job. From a professional point of view, he had a desire to extend the range of his performance whatever it might require; he had no wish to become a clothes

In his most famous role as Indiana Jones in *Raiders of the Lost Ark*
(*Lucasfilm Limited/Paramount*)

Indiana Jones seeking the Ark and (below) on the verge of discovering it (*Lucasfilm Limited/Paramount*)

Harrison Ford at the 1981 Deauville Festival of American films where
Raiders was shown (*Rex Features*)

As Rick Deckard in the futuristic thriller *Blade Runner* (*Rex Features*)

Ford as Rick Deckard on the run from murderous replicant, Roy Batty in *Blade Runner* (*Ladd Co./Warner Brothers*)

On the set of *Blade Runner* with director Ridley Scott (*Ladd Co./Warner Brothers*)

Deckard fighting for his life, *Blade Runner* (*Ladd Co./Warner Brothers*)

Ford with co-star Mark Hamill in *Return of the Jedi* (*Lucasfilm Limited/ Twentieth Century Fox*)

The *Return of the Jedi* team: George Lucas (far left), director Richard Marquand (far right), and the cast, back row: Harrison Ford, Carrie Fisher, Mark Hamill. Front row: Anthony Daniels (C-3PO), Kenny Baker (R2-D2) and Peter Mayhew (Chewbacca) (*Lucasfilm Limited/Twentieth Century Fox*)

Harrison Ford with his wife Melissa Matheson at the Deauville Film Festival in 1982 (*Rex Features*)

horse that talked and moved in all the right places. He also had a perfect understanding of the character of Indiana Jones and what that required of him: 'He does brave things,' he observed. 'He teaches, but I wouldn't describe him as an intellectual. He doesn't have any fancy gadgetry keeping him at a distance from enemies and trouble. He's right in there with just a bullwhip to keep the world at bay.' Ford too, wanted to be 'right in there' to play his part.

It was not as easy as it looked, however. Jones *is* a very physical character, unlike any Ford had played before, and the story involved him in events rather than individual exploits. The demands that were placed upon Ford seemed at times to overstep the bounds of sense. 'Boy, does that guy get bruised,' he remembered. 'That's why people like him so much. He gets hurt, see? Everyone can identify with him. But he's determined, which is why I like him. He just won't give up, whatever they throw at him.'

This reveals a great deal about Harrison Ford's character. The single-mindedness and determination that are perhaps the most significant of his own personal qualities were reflected in and embodied by the adventurous exploits of Indiana Jones. 'There's a lot of me in him,' he has admitted, 'in my mind.' What Ford may or may not have realized is that Jones nearly always succeeds *despite* himself: he fails spectacularly in the opening sequence, and is lucky to escape with his life; he gains and loses the Ark, and only retrieves it after its powers destroy the Nazis, all of which would have happened whether Jones was there or not. In all the important scenes he is a *passive* participant, in that he is always a pawn in the action rather than any kind of instigator of it. It is perhaps that ambivalence, the fact that Jones appears to be a great adventurer, but is in truth as flawed and reliant upon Chance as the rest of us, that makes him so appealing. After all, he loses the Ark in the end, but he does get the girl.

The stunts in which Ford is involved are the most immediately impressive feature of the film. The actor was sufficiently able in their performance to prompt Martin Grace, one of the principal stuntmen and doubles for the film, to comment: 'With guidance he can do a lot. A little instruction on the detail and he's there.' Nonetheless, Ford was sufficiently realistic to appreciate the disadvantages of such involvement: 'When I'm not too sore, I enjoy it,' he told Derek Taylor. 'You get a lot of bumps doing movie-magic, even with stuntmen taking their shares. A bump here and a bump there add up to a bruised and battered body. You can do a lot of the stuff yourself, and I'm glad to if the stunt is co-ordinated so that there is an advantage for the film in my doing it myself. I don't want to do it for the glory. But sometimes I begin to feel more like a football player, a *battered* football player, than a movie actor.'

There were various incidents during filming which show just how dangerous Ford's stunts were. On one occasion, during the scene depicting Indy's fight with a German underneath the Flying Wing aeroplane, he came as close to serious injury as he ever wanted: 'Everybody's ready and the take begins,' he told *Prevue* magazine. 'I go down and start to roll away, and my foot slips right under the rolling 'plane's tyre. Everybody was yelling "Stop! Stop!" while the tyre crawled up my leg. Luckily the brakes worked – inches before my knee was crushed – but I was pinned to the sand. I'm not normally a worrier, I know they're not going to kill the main character in a twenty-million-dollar film. I also know Indy wouldn't look good with a peg leg. I was a lot more careful about stunt work after that!'

The actor's flippant remark reveals less than the fact that he continued to take part in any stunts that were required of him, despite his near-accident. Like Jones, Harrison Ford is not a man to be daunted by a little adversity, whatever form it may take. During filming in Tunisia, for example, Ford contracted severe diarrhoea, and felt about as far removed from his man-of-action role as was possible. He was still on set for the 6 a.m. roll-call, however.

Also like Jones, Ford's particularly individual approach always carried him through, and he was often instrumental in steering the film over sticky patches. 'Harrison is a very original leading man,' observed Steven Spielberg. 'There's not been anyone like him for thirty or forty years, and he does carry the movie wonderfully. Harrison was more than just an actor playing a role, he was a collaborator and really was involved in a lot of decision-making about the movie. And this wasn't by contract, it was because I sensed a very good story mind and a real smart person, and called on him time and again.'

That good story mind came to the fore in perhaps the most entertaining scene in the movie, where Indy decides to shoot an awesome Arab swordsman who threatens him in the marketplace. Spielberg had actually shot a sequence of the two fighting, a short section of which can be seen in the *Making of Raiders of the Lost Ark* television special, and was preparing to continue with the scene, when Ford suggested they should 'shoot the sucker instead'. The idea immediately appealed to Spielberg: apart from saving time and money, it was also more appropriate to Indy's state of mind. As Ford explained: 'It was the right thing for the character to do at that moment in time. All he cares about is finding Marion, and if he can avoid another fight and get to her that much quicker, he's gonna do it. He wouldn't have given the guy an even break. And I felt that Indiana, because it's the only time he ever shoots anybody in cold blood, I felt that the audience would forgive him for that, because he is fighting for truth, justice and the American way. And I never really assumed that that would be considered a flaw in his character, or even a criminal action. Certainly the whip against the sword was a bad match, and if I were ever in his position and there was a girl whose life was in immediate danger, I would probably have done the same thing.'

It seems that it was primarily Harrison Ford's interpretation and understanding of the character that drove the film along, even though he underplayed the extent of his influence. 'There's a lot of gritty action in *Raiders*,' he commented, 'but you have to remember – it's only make-believe. . . Much of its success is due to the affectionate tribute it pays to the past.' Others, however, appreciated the degree to which he had brought the character to life, and had infused the movie with a moral logic and vitality of its own. Writer Lawrence Kasdan in particular, perhaps the only man who knew Indiana Jones better than George Lucas, enthused about Ford's performance. 'One of my great delights about Indiana Jones,' he told James H. Burns, 'is the way in which Harrison Ford brought him to life. Harrison has great charisma without being cocky, and shows that he's a real movie star. . . I'm thrilled with him in *Raiders* because I was one of the people who wasn't crazy about him in *Empire*. In *Raiders* he's shockingly good.'

The rest of the world seemed to agree. Though in many countries it was to meet with censorship and criticism of the violence it portrayed, on its release in the United States on 12 July 1981, the film outshone even *Star Wars* in terms of popularity. By 1986 it had earned over $375 million in ticket sales worldwide, and had made Harrison Ford's bank manager very happy indeed: Ford's position in the film industry had allowed him to negotiate for seven per cent of profits. *Raiders* also reaffirmed his status as a leading cinema actor. The hero had returned – this time for good.

The final word of this chapter should be left to Ford himself, who described just what the film and his involvement with Lucas meant to him: 'If it wasn't for George, I'd still be building furniture.'

Now he was building a career.

7

Future Tense

Ford's growing reputation in the film world as a skilled and innovative actor led him next to his involvement with the meticulously futuristic *Blade Runner*. This film provided him with one of his most challenging parts to date; an opportunity to bring to his performance a more subtle array of qualities than his previous roles had allowed him. This was a film which consciously broke new ground. Producer Alan Ladd Jnr said it was 'Futuristic, I guess. Science Future I guess is closer to it', which was perhaps the most accurate of all the attempts to describe the film. Ford's own, 'An old tale with new twists and wrinkles', took the prize for the most tantalisingly prosaic.

It was to be directed by Ridley Scott, whose work on *The Duellists* and *Alien* had elevated him to the top stratum of directors after an apprenticeship served in the cause of English advertisements. Twentieth Century Fox had already set the pre-production ball in motion, without any particular director in mind, when Sandy Lieberson suggested Scott as helmsman, and the studio approved. Michael Deeley approached the director with a suggested script and, although his acceptance was not immediate, Scott's unique ability to visualize a project in its most dynamic form lead him to agree to handle it. 'I was working on *Alien* when I first read the *Blade Runner* script, and it made me curious. I wondered if that kind of hell can happen in space, what would the cities be like?' he told

Prevue magazine. 'At first I wasn't sure I wanted to do it. I'd just finished one science fiction film and didn't particularly care to do another. Of course, I realised it wasn't *really* science fiction, but a detective-adventure story, a film set forty years hence presented in the style of forty years ago. It was the type of project which allowed me to develop the exotic areas that interest me, yet still do an earthbound, near-contemporary film.'

The original source for the film was the Philip K. Dick novel *Do Androids Dream Of Electric Sheep?*, long recognized as a science fiction classic and for just as long considered unfilmable in its natural state. It was a problem that Scott readily acknowledged. 'The film itself has a slight resemblance to the novel,' he told *Starlog*. 'The Dick novel is very complex, very convoluted. A brilliant piece which in book form would never make a film. It's too complex, a very special piece of literature.'

This complexity, although assimilated and carefully interpreted for the film, was reflected in the various stages of the project's development. Originally, Jay Cocks and Martin Scorcese, director of *Taxi Driver* and *Alice Doesn't Live Here Anymore*, had shown an interest in developing the book as a film, but they decided not to purchase the film rights. Then, as author Philip K. Dick told *Starlog*, 'Herb Jaffe optioned it and Robert Jaffe did a screenplay back about 1973. The screenplay was sent to me and it was so crude that I didn't understand that it was actually the shooting script. I thought it was a rough. I wrote to them and asked them if they would like me to do the shooting script, at which point Robert Jaffe flew down here to Orange County and confessed that he had written it under a *nom de plume*. I said to him then that it was so bad that I wanted to know if he wanted me to beat him up there at the airport, or wait until we got to my apartment.'

The different perceptions of the project held by the Jaffes and Dick, whose obvious nearness to his own creation contrasted with the Jaffes' idea of the way the film world does its business, were never really resolved. 'I said that I'd honestly prefer to buy back the property than let him make a film based on that property,' said Dick, 'and he was real nice about it. I gave him suggestions, and he took notes, and then I noticed that he wasn't actually writing, but rather he was just moving the pen about a quarter of an inch from a piece of paper that already had printing on it, so that he was only pretending to take notes. I realized then that there was a gulf between me and Hollywood.'

Fortunately, they remained good friends whilst agreeing to differ, and in 1977 the Jaffes allowed their option on the project to lapse. This suited screenwriters Hampton Fancher and Brian Kelly, who purchased the rights to the film, following up an interest Fancher had expressed to Dick in the mid-seventies. At that meeting, Dick had been reticent about dealing with Fancher because the property was already under option, but he soon discovered that the two of them worked particularly well together; their respective ideas of what were the important themes and stresses of the novel seemed to be closely matched.

Unfortunately, the first script, produced by Fancher, who never really intended to be the writer on the project anyway, was not rated at all highly by Dick. 'They aimed low and they failed at what they aimed at,' he told *Starlog*. It looked like the less than successful episode with the Jaffes might be repeated. However, the introduction of screenwriter David Peoples to the project totally reversed the situation. 'That guy's a genius,' said Dick. 'Now the book and the screenplay form two parts of a single whole. . . This is a miracle, a real miracle.' One part Peoples changed was Fancher's ending, in which Deckard convinced Rachael to commit suicide – an idea which Dick thought missed much of the book's original thrust. But Peoples was characteristically generous in his praise of Fancher's efforts. 'I don't know which ones Phil Dick read that he didn't like, but certainly the one I read was absolutely brilliant,' he said.

By this time the film had undergone two name changes – from the novel's original title to a simple 'The Android', and then 'Dangerous Days' – and Michael Deeley had managed to set up a production deal with Filmways. Unfortunately, it was a relationship which failed to get much further than an initial agreement. As the proposed budget for the film escalated, Filmways found the responsibilities of a $15 million-plus production too heavy a weight to bear, and they withdrew a couple of months before principle photography was scheduled to begin. However, with typical dexterity, Deeley managed to turn everything around and obtained backing from The Ladd Company, which further pleased Philip K. Dick for he found himself dealing with people who were genuinely interested in what he had to say.

Alan Ladd Jnr was the man who had financed *Star Wars*. He had also produced Ridley Scott's *Alien*, so it seemed that the whole *Blade Runner* project was destined to come under his wing. In co-operation, appropriately enough, with Tandem Productions the Ladd Company agreed to fund what was rapidly becoming a $25 million production.

The most pressing task now was to find someone to play the multi-faceted lead role of Rick Deckard. Harrison Ford had been approached during the shooting of *The Empire Strikes Back* but he had found the project unappealing, and for one particular reason: 'They were going to make it in London at that point in their plans,' he told Alan McKenzie, 'and I said, "Well, thank you very much, gentlemen, but I don't want to work in London any more. I want to go home".' This was a point he pursued in a later *Face* interview: 'I've had the same dressing room at Elstree for four films and it's beginning to feel pretty old. This is a wonderful country, very pretty, and I admire the people, but London is obviously a tourist economy and I'm quite prey to it. Generally, it ain't what it used to be, is it?'

Ford had always been Ridley Scott's first choice for the role. 'I just knew he was right for it,' he told *Photoplay*. 'It's a departure from what he's done before because the character has more depth than the ones he usually plays. I've always thought he was a fine actor.' But Ford's refusal of the part meant that Scott was forced to spread his net a little wider. At one point Dustin Hoffman was approached, which points to the somewhat fluid nature of the project, and the difficulty those involved had in tying it down. Hoffman expressed surprise at being considered for such a role. It may be that Scott, unable to get his first choice, did not want to take a Harrison Ford 'clone', and so went for a completely different type of character. Though the liaison threw up many fine ideas, not least from Hoffman, the idea eventually fell through.

When the Ladd Company became involved with the production, the planned centre of operations for the film was moved from London to Hollywood. Ford was approached again, this time with more success. His initial objection removed, he accepted the role of Deckard, negotiating a twenty per cent profit-sharing deal in the process. 'I ask and they pay,' he noted, underlining his growing bankability.

His decision was to prove significant not only in the

development of the central character, but also in the conception of the film as a whole. 'Harrison has an immense understanding of the entire movie-making process,' Ridley Scott told Milo Mitchell. 'You can't fool him at all – he always knows *exactly* what's happening. His contributions were tremendous, on a story level as well as to his own character. He brought many ideas to me. In fact, it got bloody embarrassing. They were so good, there was *no way* I could wriggle out of using them. For example, Harrison figured he should go for utter reality, almost like De Niro's Travis Bickle in *Taxi Driver* – the substance of the central character was *essential*. Harrison developed and kept it that way. He takes full credit for that, not me.'

It is clear that Scott's vision of the character was inextricably bound up with his perception of Ford's abilities as an actor. 'He has a very unusual quality . . . a strange, slightly sinister side, very low key and sombre, almost a *different* Harrison Ford. Very dangerous. It fits the nature of both Deckard and the film very well.'

It is also apparent that Ford had a similar respect for Scott's work and harboured equally high hopes for the film. He told *Films* magazine that he saw it as 'an important step towards more serious roles. . . I was serious about it because of the people involved and was happy to find out that Ridley was interested in developing the density of the characters as well. I felt that we could work together to present a character who was interesting and very different to anything else I've done until now.'

This perception of the role as one which afforded a greater range than his previous work was something he constantly reiterated. 'It's totally unlike anything I've ever done before,' he said. 'The story has an element of psychological drama I've never dealt with before in a film, and it takes place in a world no one has ever seen.'

Unfortunately, some of Scott's comments about his approach to films indicate a possible source of contention between himself and Harrison Ford. Where Ford saw the actor as instrumental in both the presentation of the film and its evolution, Scott saw things from a slightly different perspective. 'There are certain moments in movies,' Scott observed, 'where the background can be as important as the actor. The design of a film *is* the script.' From a visual stylist's point of view it was an obvious statement to make; from that of an actor like Harrison Ford it was just plain wrong. Pretty pictures do not an interesting film make.

Ridley Scott's ideas for the visualization of this world no one has ever seen were as precise and meticulous as those underpinning his two previous films, and he knew instinctively what he wanted to achieve. 'The city we present is overkill,' he told *Cinefex* magazine, 'but I always get the impression of New York being overkill. You go into New York on a bad day, and you look around, and you feel this place is going to grind to a halt any minute – which it nearly does all too often.' However, any notions that the film was going to turn into an exercise in USA-phobia were quickly dispelled. Scott's idea was to present a Chandleresque science fiction film, a forties-style homage to a future not yet contemplated, with a single anti-hero against the oppressive megalopolis – not the easiest ambition to achieve. The anti-hero who never plays by the rules, who only takes part in the game at all because of the need to survive, is a common enough theme in Hollywood cinema. It can be traced back to Marlowe and beyond, through the kind of rogueish male leads so often played by Errol Flynn.

101

What was required for the film to have any chance of success was a team of individuals able to conceptualize Scott's idiosyncratic vision of the future. One member of the team he hired was a designer called Syd Mead. 'About three years ago, I bought a book called *Sentinel*,' explained Scott, 'which was Syd Mead's book, and which was really very interesting because it had *very* exotic projections about vehicles and industrial design – done for everyone from General Motors to washing machine companies to computer manufacturers. What I especially liked was the fact Syd Mead's future seemed to be well grounded in logic, and that's what I wanted for *Blade Runner*. I wanted it to be futuristic without being silly.'

This need for credibility was something that Mead also appreciated. 'When you're creating an artificial reality, you can't get too far out. You have to do what the audience believes is probably the way the things would look. All the elements have to look like they belong where they are, and they have to explain themselves as they flash by. Otherwise it doesn't work, and it puts a roadblock in the way of the story.'

Scott began to arrange around him a host of gifted designers and technicians as well as Mead, including Douglas Trumbull, who had worked on *2001* and *Star Trek – The Movie*, and who had directed *Silent Running*; his partner, Richard Yuricich; Jordan Cronenweth; David Dryer; Matthew Yuricich, *et al*. If Ford had harboured any hidden qualms about working on the project, the inclusion of such gifted and imaginative people, all of whom he considered masters of their craft, quickly put them to flight. Unusually for an actor, he was able to appreciate the talents they brought to bear on the film from the standpoint of the craftsmanship they exhibited. His interest in carpentry had not lessened, though the pressures of film work had meant he did not practice it as often as he liked, and he often chose to spend time with the designers and technicians discovering and discussing just what was going on.

The set chosen was Warner Brothers' famous New York Street at the Burbank Studios, scene of many classic forties detective films, but now re-dressed to match Ridley Scott's vision of Los Angeles in 2019. 'Films usually attempt to do the future by presenting a rather bleak, pristine, austere, clean look,' he told *American Cinematographer*. 'It could go that way, but I've got a feeling it's going to go the other way.' To obtain this, Syd Mead's 'retro-fitted' idea, of 'smacking things on the outside' to get 'a picture of a textured city' was given free rein.

The realization of this grandiloquent vision required an unswerving attention to detail on the part of Scott, who had an overwhelmingly personal eye for the project. 'I *know* what I want,' he told *Prevue* magazine. 'I go for the very best people I can, and put them under a lot of pressure. Sometimes they don't like it but, later, they'll enjoy the end result because it's *right*. That's what counts.'

But what was Ford's response to the kind of pressure Scott put him under? In the *Souvenir* magazine, he described the scene where Deckard shoots at Batty: 'If you sit down and analyze it, there are probably twenty contingent factors that all have to be right at the same time to make that scene work. Ridley demands that of himself and of everybody else. It's not an easy task, but that's what I like. I like to work hard, and I like to work for somebody who is exacting and sure of himself.'

The obvious danger was that Scott's concern for the minutiae of the film's production would obscure the need for character development in the movie, but in this department,

103

Ford's help was invaluable. I already knew when I began the film that I had Harrison Ford,' Scott told *Cinema* magazine. 'His film *Raiders of the Lost Ark* hadn't come out yet. In fact, they were just finishing it in England when I met him. He was the bedraggled Indiana Jones who had, in fact, many of the elements that I had originally wanted in *Blade Runner*. I wanted a guy with a Bogart hat, the slightly unshaven appearance, the slightly long hair, but he said "You can't do that – I'm doing that right now". So instead we made him look like Elvis Costello.'

Initially, therefore, the actual physical appearance of the character relied very much upon Ford's own ideas, a fact which he explained in *The Souvenir* magazine. 'The haircut was my idea. Ridley had envisioned a big felt hat in his first visual concept of the character at a time prior to seeing *Raiders of the Lost Ark*. It was important to me not to wear the same hat in one movie after another. I didn't want to drag the baggage of one project to the next. You can't do that. So the hat was out. Ridley still wanted something to distinguish the character and wanted something easy-care. So I got that haircut, figuring it would give the character definition, a certain look.'

This look was assimilated by Ford into his idea of the kind of man Deckard must be. The 'reluctant detective who dresses like a middle-aged Elvis Costello' is also a 'skilled investigator, an expert in his field, but he's a little out of practice when the story opens. He's lost his motor-drive. Exterminating people, even non-human ones, is not something he likes to do, and he's not comfortable with authority. He's very tough, but he's no match for a top-of-the-line replicant.'

In simple terms, Deckard had grown weary of life, grown tired of killing others in order that he might survive. It was a feeling with which Harrison Ford felt he might at least marginally associate. The need to compromise oneself in order simply to get on with life had been, a stumbling block he had come across many times in his early career. It was also a course which he had chosen to reject, and perhaps because of that, he was to bring a particular and individual understanding to the part.

To play opposite Ford in the role of Rachael, the replicant with disturbingly human emotions, the team chose the beautiful Sean Young, who had been seen previously as a military policeman in *Stripes*. 'I had seen Sean Young's photograph on my wall nine months before we started shooting,' producer Michael Deeley told the *Souvenir* magazine. 'She was always thought of as a possible Rachael, but she seemed too young. Then we screen-tested, and everyone's concept of what Rachael should look like came true. On the screen she is extremely sophisticated, and looks breathtaking.'

Young's concept of the film is interesting in the way it reflects the ideas of Ford and Scott, but changes the emphasis. 'To me this is a romance, a love story,' she said. 'I didn't approach this as science fiction. It's a romantic thriller, like *Casablanca*. But instead of Africa we're in the future.' The quality she brought to the part was to act as a foil to Ford's downbeat detective to particular effect. However, she reportedly found her co-star 'probably an all-or-nothing type of person, unable really to relate to other cast members full out, because he feels he might become wrapped up'. Ford's dedication and professionalism seemed to give rise to a rather cold personality, as perceived by his fellow actors, but it was probably more his absolute determination to make the best possible job of his involvement with the film that caused this, rather than any feelings of antagonism or superiority. He and Young got on sufficiently well to produce an absolutely con-

105

vincing, and truly poignant portrayal of the developing relationship between Rachael and Deckard. In fact, they acted so well that various rumours circulated during production that they were having an affair. It was a charge Ford never even bothered to respond to, and considering some of Young's remarks about him, it seems more than unlikely that they contained any truth.

Roy Batty, a 'goddam one-man fighting machine,' as Police Chief Bryant calls him, and really the means to Deckard's end, was played by Dutch actor Rutger Hauer. 'Ridley had seen me in *Nighthawks* and *Soldier of Orange*,' Hauer told *Starlog*, 'and then he saw some other film I did and he wanted me. That's how it started.' His on-set involvement with Harrison Ford proved to be fairly infrequent, and he does not seem to have encountered any difficulties. 'I only had two moments in the film with him,' he explained, 'and so I didn't work that long with him, but he was fine. . . Our scenes were very clearly written in the script, and so I didn't feel that problem of communication because we didn't have to talk about it.' It should be remembered, however, that Hauer has a similar reputation for professionalism that borders on disdain, and his comments on Ford should be taken in that context.

Daryl Hannah, later to star in the highly successful comedy *Splash*, was chosen as Batty's fellow replicant, Pris, a surreal lover and compatriot. Joanna Cassidy, later of *Under Fire* and the *Buffalo Bill* television series, was chosen as Zhora, the replicant with strength as well as beauty. And Brion James played Leon, whose mental level may have been set at 'C' by his creators, but whose ability for raw violence almost costs Deckard his life. Ably abetted by Joe Turkel, William Sanderson, M. Emmett Walsh and Edward James Olmos, amongst others, the casting jigsaw finally came together.

Finally, after all the re-writes and conflicts, the casting problems, financial pressures and doubts about the viability of the project, the film was ready to be set in motion. In March 1981, approximately seven years after Hampton Fancher had first contacted Philip K. Dick with a view to obtaining the film rights, the now re-titled *Blade Runner* went into production. The final name-change had been instigated by Fancher and came from a novel by Alan Nourse, the rights of which the producers were forced to buy in order to be able to use it. And then, in the convoluted fashion to which all associated with the project were now becoming accustomed, they discovered that the William Burrough's film script for the novel, though never realized on the big screen, had been turned into a novel by Burroughs and published. The rights to that version had also to be purchased before things were ready to proceed.

Scott had arranged around him a team of craftsmen who were not only highly gifted, but who were also completely committed to the project, and he was able to develop his thematic overview in an atmosphere of mutual respect and dedication. Harrison Ford's contribution to the picture was particularly appreciated by all concerned. Associate producer Ivor Powell described the actor's involvement to Alan McKenzie of *Starburst*: 'I think he's wonderful, number one for me. Very professional. . . He loves his craft and has no delusions of grandeur about him at all, and he's great to work with. He has a very positive in-put on script, on how to do action scenes – terrific.'

Over a period of four months, the film team created a claustrophobic vision of Los Angeles in the year 2019 AD, with mythological references ranging from Tyrell's vast pyramidic edifice to Batty's metaphorical self-crucifixion. In July 1981, only slightly over schedule and budget, *Blade Runner* was completed. There could be little doubt that this was one of the most eloquent films ever made in the science fiction genre. From the awesome opening cityscape scenes, to the image of flame washing around the pupil of an eye, and the final, desperate slamming of the lift doors – all underscored by the flawless Vangelis soundtrack – the effect was staggering.

The original cut of the film, about fifteen minutes longer than the final version, was previewed in Denver and Dallas, with unfavourable audience reaction. Some people seemed to find it hard to accept Harrison Ford as anything less than an all-muscle action man. The very point that seemed to fascinate Ford about the film – the developing dichotomy between what is supposedly human and non-human, and the way human and replicant behaviour begins to contradict moral expectations – was lost on many. And this was despite the fact that Ridley Scott had avoided the trap of favouring style over content, and had presented an adventure thriller of sorts.

The film was quickly re-cut, a more extensive voice-over was provided, action scenes were tightened up, and, perhaps most incredibly of all, a happy ending concocted from movie jetsam was tacked on. The end scenes of Ford in his speedster with Sean Young were intercut with out-takes from Kubrick's *The Shining*, completely changing the emphasis of the original. Deckard's final scene with Batty, though still highly charged in the re-cut, was absolutely heartrending in the original, in which Ford says simply, 'I sat for six hours and watched him die'.

Ford avoided being drawn into any criticism about the film. 'I never expect to be completely pleased by anything I do, because by nature I'm a perfectionist,' he told Jane Goodwin. 'I'm afraid we're going to exceed my capacity for frankness

108

very soon if we discuss *Blade Runner*. I got a lot of enjoyment out of doing the work itself, but the end result was pretty much out of my hands after a certain point, so I might as well put it out of my mouth as well.'

When pushed, Ridley Scott expressed similar indeterminate reservations about the film. '*Blade Runner* was a monolithic task,' he told *Starlog* magazine. 'It was murderous to do, and I think I *was* disappointed with it. But I wasn't surprised, because I knew I hadn't quite got it, and I knew I had lost aspects that I originally had set out to do. The reasons how and why I lost things, I'm *not* going to say. . . I was disappointed because anything you do, it's a killer. . . I thought *Blade Runner* was a good movie except for a couple of things I would like to have changed. . . On reflection it has all slowly crawled back up the hill. Anyway, what do you expect – we came out the same time as *E.T.*' Harrison Ford and Ridley Scott parted company on cold, if mutually respectful terms.

The film was not the great commercial success that had been hoped for, perhaps because of the kind of limited expectations that the audiences in the preview shows had exhibited. On opening it took a disappointing $6,150,002 in 1,295 theatres. The kind of pre-conditioning that the *Star Wars* films and *Raiders of the Lost Ark* had worked upon the audience's collective subconscious seemed to scare them away from a film that actually made them think. Ford's characterization threw up questions about life and death, human relationships and morality which his previous roles had never explored in any depth. Deckard lives in a world he cannot control and will never conquer, certainly not by the daring exploits or dab-hand heroics of an Indiana Jones or a Han Solo. It is his recognition of this fact that makes him the most human, and therefore the most complex character Ford had yet portrayed.

Working with Ridley Scott, an intensely creative director with incredible attention to detail, and an unswerving grasp of his own visualization of the film's development, was also a new experience for Ford. Unlike the films with Spielberg and Lucas, both of whom he knew very well, Ford had to work in an unfamiliar situation and gain himself the freedom to explore and develop his character without undermining the rest of the film. The fact that he accomplished this with such success serves to highlight the extent of his development as an actor and a dedicated professional.

His performance in the central role proved to be quite outstanding. Probably his most complex characterization to date, Ford responded to its various challenges with all guns blazing, a fact acknowledged by Ridley Scott. 'I knew Rick Deckard, the central character of *Blade Runner*, was so different from Han Solo that it represented a kind of challenge to Harrison,' he told journalist Robert Greenberger. 'He would most certainly have played against the central character that we know him for, plus the fact that, from my point of view as a film-maker and someone who is actually trying to aim a movie at an audience, people were familiar with Harrison. I knew it was double-edged. It was a great choice, you know, because I knew Harrison wanted a change of pace, and he certainly has done that.'

Associate producer Ivor Powell, similarly enamoured of Ford's performance, told *Starburst*: 'He understands film-making and how to make a dodgy scene seem good. I think he is called upon to perform, to act more in *Blade Runner* than in anything else I've seen him in, certainly more than *Star Wars*. I think it's a very difficult performance . . . a very difficult part to play, because on the one hand as *Blade Runner* is a big, commercial action movie, you can't devote the time to characterization and development to scenes that you could do in a smaller movie.'

Perhaps the most impressive praise of all came from author Philip K. Dick, whose perception of the character of Deckard was probably the hardest of all to live up to. 'Harrison Ford is more like Rick Deckard than I could have ever imagined,' he told the *Souvenir* magazine. 'I mean, it is just incredible. It was simply eerie when I first saw the stills of Harrison Ford. I was looking at some stills from the movie, and I thought, this character really exists. There was a time that he did not exist, now he actually exists. . . Ford radiates this tremendous reality when you see him. And seeing him as a character I created is a stunning and almost supernatural experience to me.'

All those concerned with the film seemed genuinely satisfied with the outcome. The original version embodied all of Dick's themes and concerns, and the film had been infused with a genuine life of its own, rather than remaining, like so many other science fiction films, merely a parody of a genre.

Perhaps the last word should be left to Philip K. Dick who, though he never saw the final cut, described the film thus: 'There's some tender parts, and there's some very intelligent parts,' he told *Starlog*. 'It's a very mature and sophisticated screenplay, and it has subtle nuances which are *very* good. It appeals not just to the dramatic – although it is very dramatic – it also appeals to the intellect.'

111

8

The End of the Empire

Harrison Ford's elevation to the level of one of the most sought-after film actors in the world brought with it different kinds of pressures. From a personal perspective, it created a need to decide precisely how to use this new-found vehicle to his best advantage. 'I'm very cautious of the word "star",' he observed to Alan McKenzie. 'I do my job. I've been very lucky. Now I have to figure how to milk it.'

This seems an unusual and uncharacteristically mercenary attitude for Ford to take. However, it is fair to assume that he was concerned less with the need to make as quick a buck as possible and more with the fact that the increase in his reputation – and bankability – meant he could regain control of his career to a significant extent. Nonetheless, the fact that Harrison Ford's name above any film caused people to queue three times around the block might have inhibited him in subsequent performances. Those difficulties surfaced in his next project.

In 1981, George Lucas began to pull together the ideas and story-lines for the third and final movie in the *Star Wars* trilogy. Provisionally entitled *Revenge of the Jedi*, the film that was to fulfil the director's 'slight compulsion to finish the story' presented few new logistical problems. There was, however, a need to recognize a certain shift in emphasis with regard to the audience's perception of the principal characters. Ford's success outside the Lucasfilm milieu had been so great that the part of Han Solo, once conceived of as a secondary, if integral supporting figure, now generated increasing attention. This could be made to work to everyone's benefit, but first of all Ford had to be convinced to play the role.

Ford proved wary of playing Han Solo for a third time. 'I just don't have the patience to do methodical, safe, repetitious, formula acting,' he told Alan McKenzie. 'I like film acting because every experience is new – new sets, new actors, new directors.' Han Solo was a lot of things, but he certainly was not new. 'I don't live out my fantasies,' said Ford, 'I choose from amongst what is offered to me at any given time. I look for parts that contrast with the last thing I've done. I don't wish to do the same thing twice, and I try to put as much distance between past characters as possible. The reason I choose something depends on a lot of things. Whether I like the people involved and think I can get along properly with them. Whether I think it's good and worthwhile to do. A lot of different elements enter into it . . . whether I want to work at that time.' Ford clearly saw the part of Han Solo in *The Return of the Jedi* as a retrograde step. Whereas his return to *The Empire Strikes Back* had offered a means of salvaging something from a rather disappointing period in his career, to take on Solo *once again* might just set him on a downward cycle. Perhaps out of a sense of loyalty to Lucas, however, he finally agreed to do it.

Once that hurdle had been overcome, a second problem surfaced. The character of Han Solo would have to be developed in such a manner that it would not imbalance the already established themes and relationships of the *Star Wars* concept. It was important that Solo did not become simply a shadowy replica of Indiana Jones, triggering inappropriate memories in the minds of fans. Ford and Lucas held detailed pre-production discussions as to what was the best course to chart, considering the delicate balance that had to be struck.

Of all the ideas and suggestions they came up with, Ford thought of the simplest and most practical solution to the problem. 'Let's kill him off,' he told Lucas, 'That'll tie it up.' Lucas' reaction was predictable: the *Star Wars* trilogy had proved such a particularly personal creation that he could not bear to bring about the demise of any of the characters. Ford disagreed. 'I thought it would give the myth some body,' he told *Time* magazine. 'Solo really had no place to go. He's got no papa, he's got no mama, he's got no story. But that was the one thing I was unable to convince George of.' It was a fairly radical step to suggest, but Ford's motives probably went further than simply selling a good story idea. By killing Solo he could bring an end to the past, and thus clear the decks for the future. Lucas, however, saw things differently.

To Lucas it was clear that the Good must be seen to triumph absolutely in his films; the fact that he was to change the name of the film from *Revenge* to *Return of the Jedi*, thus avoiding the original's negative associations, was another example of this. Dale Pollock records that Lucas observed that, 'The whole emotion I am trying to get at the end of this film is for you to be emotionally and spiritually uplifted, and to feel absolutely good about life. That is the greatest thing that we could ever possibly do.'

Unfortunately human beings are not spiritually uplifted by everything being as sweet and artificial as chocolate cake: they become so by triumphing over adversity. Ford's suggestion that Solo should die revealed a fine perception of that fact. If Luke and Leia had won through, but the reality of loss in life had been embodied by Solo's death, the films as a whole would have had a far greater relevance and moral

115

range. This is because the three central characters would have experienced almost all it is possible for human beings to experience. Thus, the *Star Wars* trilogy would have succeeded as a body of work, as Lucas had always professed he wanted it to, rather than being three films strung together by various plot devices. The characters would have been seen to grow, to mature to a realization that their own personal needs were outweighed by something higher, though that something might have been different in each case. In all, the films would have acquired additional depth and subtlety.

But it was not to be. Han Solo, once the mercenary outlaw whose love of money was only outweighed by his love for himself, became another goody-goody. The heart of gold was shown to be nothing more than chocolate wrapped in shiny foil. And anyone who falls in love with a princess *has* to be a total square.

Once Lucas had made his position clear, however, Ford turned his attentions to fulfilling the director's perceptions of a character that had become an integral feature of his past. 'If I hadn't been able to do some of my other movies I might have felt differently about doing *Return of the Jedi,*' he told Tony Crawley. 'As it stands, I'm delighted to be coming back. Han, Luke and Princess Leia were created to tell this story, so I'm glad to be in on the third act.'

From the way Ford explained his involvement in the film, it is clear that it was primarily out of a sense of loyalty to Lucas, the man who made him a star, that he agreed to play Solo one last time. He did not feel any great association with the character, despite the fact that for many of his fans it was the part he was born to play. All in all, the *Star Wars* trilogy was just a little too long for an actor constantly seeking new ground and fresh challenges. However, Harrison Ford was now back in the Lucasfilm fold – producer Howard Kazanjian, when asked if it had been difficult to get the actor back, replied, 'Back where?' – and *Return of the Jedi* was ready to roll.

It had taken George Lucas only four weeks to write the story, possibly because it had been distilling in his mind for twelve years. Now that he had his principal actors, he needed someone to pull the whole thing together and give it all a definite shape. Once again, he looked to a familiar face for the help he needed. In the October 1981 issue of *Starlog* magazine, Lawrence Kasdan had categorically stated, 'I don't know what my future will hold for me in *any* way. I can say, though, that I won't be writing the next Star Wars film.' Yet, in the 'Stop Press' of the same magazine, he had to admit, 'It's a big surprise to me that I'm writing *Revenge of the Jedi*'. Lucas' famed persuasive powers had worked again. The project had become so important to him that, as with Ford, he wanted someone on whom he knew he could totally rely. Kasdan had pulled *Empire* out of the fire, and had turned *Raiders* into a perfect realization of Lucas' dream, and he knew that *Return of the Jedi* needed similar treatment. Like the proverbial Canadian Mountie, he always got his man. 'What happened is that George called me on the 'phone – we often talk with each other – and asked me to do the script as a favour to him,' Kasdan told *Starlog*. 'I told George that I hadn't planned on doing anymore "just writing" on films. He said "Aw, come on". . . I'm doing the script because I feel that I owe George a lot.'

Having succeeded in that department, Lucas went looking for the appropriate director. At one stage he even considered taking on the job himself. He realized that *Return of the Jedi* would prove to be the most important episode in the *Star Wars* sequence: if this one did not work, nor would the trilogy

117

as a whole. Numerous rumours circulated as to who would be chosen, ranging from the ubiquitous Steven Spielberg to various associates Lucas knew from film school – all inaccurate. After some consideration, Lucas decided upon Richard Marquand, a successful television director who had moved on to feature films with *The Legacy,* and the Donald Sutherland movie *The Eye of the Needle.* He appealed to Lucas because he exhibited the same aptitude for getting the story across quickly and effectively that Lucas himself considered essential for a successful film.

The two men met in January 1981, when Marquand was told for the first time that he was up for the job. 'George said I wouldn't hear for a while,' he told Alan McKenzie, 'as there were other directors on the list. He had to see everybody's work. But he wanted to see everything I had done, and I said *"Please,* not everything", and he said, "Yeah, everything!". . . He was looking for someone who could work well, work fast, handle a well-established cast, was a fan of the series, who could think quickly because he had to keep the budget in check. . . He wanted someone who would interpret him. I had to know what the whole thing meant to him so I could do my job.'

It was essential to Lucas that he employed someone who could handle such gifted but at times idiosyncratic actors as Ford, Hamill and Fisher. The trio of characters had already been established in the cinema, but the personal relationships between the three became similarly fixed. Thus Marquand had to know not only exactly where the film was going, but also the personal qualities and individual capabilities of the people with whom he was involved. In an interview with Alan McKenzie, he revealed an astute recognition of the situation with which he was faced: 'Mark's character is the one that develops through the whole series. That's the area of jeopardy. Will Luke move towards the Dark Side of the Force. . ? In the last movie, Carrie Fisher's Princess became such a bitch, she really was a drag. I was sure there was a lot more depth there we could use. And more comedy, too. Turn her into more of a woman . . . and Harrison Ford's great, he really is. He's a very professional actor. A man who is quite a major box-office star. He gets on with it. Doesn't suffer fools gladly.'

The way Marquand talked about Ford, it was clear that from the beginning he had to make use of Ford's particular strengths and abilities to carry the film through. Solo was the most important character in the resolution of the *Star Wars* saga – he had already had his best shot in the first two films – but Marquand saw that this would allow Ford a freer rein to contribute his valuable ideas.

Marquand also picked up Ford's idea of having Han Solo killed, as did Lawrence Kasdan, and he continued to argue the point with Lucas in twelve-hour-a-day script discussions during early 1981. Unfortunately, Lucas continued to refuse to be swayed from his singular vision of the total triumph of Good in the film. This was to be a Lucasfilm production through and through. Lucas was even financing it with his own money: a cool $32.5 million.

Almost despite himself, Lucas had become a wealthy Hollywood mogul, and the tensions and pressures that rose out of having to use his own money to finance the production probably limited the risks he was prepared to take. Put simply, happy endings make more money, and Lucas had no wish to alienate the large percentage of the *Star Wars* audience who associated most closely with the role played by Harrison Ford.

119

Finally, on Monday 11 January 1982, the Lucasfilm entourage once again set up camp at Elstree Studios in England. The sets for the film's production were impressive: all Elstree's nine sound stages were usurped to contain everything from the swamps of Dagobah to a full-scale version of Han Solo's Millenium Falcon. It was organised chaos.

Over a period of seventy-eight days, the final instalment of *Star Wars* evolved, though not to completely uncritical acclaim. *Skywalkin'* records how one member of the film crew finally succumbed to boredom and observed, 'Someday I want to work on a movie that makes you think'. It was a little harsh: Lucas' overwhelming control of his projects might preclude too much individual initiative, but he had built up one of the most accomplished film crews in the world. It did, however, throw up the question of how far Harrison Ford might become bored with the whole affair; would he be able to respond to the demands of his character and of the actors around him, especially remembering his previous comments on the part. But as Richard Marquand observed in *Collector's* magazine, he quickly resumed the special relationship with his co-stars that had characterized Lucas' previous creation: 'I have to say that we had a tremendous group of actors. The ones playing people, I mean. I think that if we had anyone who was egocentric or waspish among the human actors, I would have been sunk. Mark Hamill, Harrison Ford and Carrie Fisher, for example, form a great club. They're ace. They really are. They've known each other and worked with each other for so long in the previous movies, that they could solve problems for me on the spot. They knew precisely where the characters were coming from, and that's such an advantage.'

The compliment was a significant one: Harrison Ford, des-

Ford returns as Indiana Jones in *Indiana Jones and the Temple of Doom*
(*Lucasfilm Limited/Paramount*)

Once again in mortal danger in *Temple of Doom*, with Ke Huy Quan (*Lucasfilm Limited/Paramount*)

Harrison Ford, George Lucas, Steven Spielberg and Kate Capshaw during the filming of *Temple of Doom* (*Lucasfilm Limited/Paramount*)

The hero is back (*Lucasfilm Limited/Paramount*)

Working on a film script at home in Hollywood (*Rex Features*)

Ford with director and friend Steven Spielberg (*Rex Features*)

Taking a break at the Cannes Film Festival (*Rex Features*)

In *Witness* Ford starred as police captain John Book, who is forced to take refuge in an Amish farm community during a murder investigation (*Paramount Pictures*)

John Book with other members of the Amish community in *Witness*
(*Paramount Pictures*)

With Alexander Godunov in a scene from *Witness* (*Paramount Pictures*)

As John Book in *Witness* wearing traditional Amish clothes (*Rex Features*)

pite his rapid elevation in the film world, was still willing and able to work within a group context without stealing anybody's fire. That openness was to prove invaluable throughout the filming, as was his advice to Marquand. Both Hamill and Fisher often seemed caught up in the roles they were playing, finding it difficult to see much beyond the immediate demands the script placed upon them. Though Marquand experienced little difficulty in working with them, it was to Ford that he turned for additional advice and suggestions.

During the shooting of *Jedi*, for the first time in the *Star Wars* trilogy, Lucas chose to carry out some location filming in the USA, a fact which Ford in particular welcomed. Though by no means parochial in outlook, he always preferred home ground to foreign parts. ('You gotta travel on, travel on,' he dispiritedly informed Jane Goodwin during interviews for *Blade Runner*). In Buttercup Valley near Yuma, Arizona the home state of Steven Spielberg, the Lucas entourage constructed sets for the planet Tattoine, and built the massive edifice which was Jabba the Hutt's sailing-barge. According to *Fantastic* magazine, the set took 110 men four months to construct, and stood 80 feet high and 212 feet long. In Crescent City, Arizona, Marquand filmed the battle scenes between imperial storm-troopers and the Rebel Alliance, scenes in which Ford was heavily involved. After thirty-five days amidst the giant redwoods that symbolized Lucas' original massive vision of *Star Wars*, *Return of the Jedi* was brought to a close.

The final scene was shot on 25 May 1982, six years and two months after filming first began on *Star Wars*, and as Richard Marquand noted in *Collector's* magazine, even the gods seemed to have smiled upon the proceedings. 'We were so

121

lucky with the weather on location. Nothing went wrong. This was supposed to be the dread season of sandstorms in Yuma. The locals were warning us, "You'll be blown out of the desert. You'll never get any shooting done. . ." But we had only two days of sandstorms when we had to stop work. And even on those days I still managed to get out and shoot some useable stuff. Not that it was easy to work. On a good day in Yuma the temperature would be a hundred and twenty degrees. That was bad for us, but for, say, the Gammorean guards in their suits, it was like running a marathon every twenty-four hours.'

During filming the cast and crew pretended to be working on a film called *Blue Harvest – Horror Beyond Imagination* in an effort to keep the project secret. It proved a pretty successful ploy. A few committed followers managed to discover the location's secret, but they were not given short shrift by Lucas, Ford and Co. Both men knew which side their bread was buttered.

Once final shooting was completed the film was removed for special effects work which took nearly a year to finalise. Lucasfilm's own Industrial Light and Magic put the finishing touches to a work that was to prove a fair testimony to Richard Marquand's ability as a director, but which relied for effect more on the impetus provided by the previous *Star Wars* instalments than on its own vitality.

On 25 May 1983 *Return of the Jedi* was unleashed upon a waiting world. But from the beginning things did not augur well. Ford, Hamill and Fisher looked far too old in their publicity pictures. Harrison Ford in particular simply looked uncomfortable in the role. He rallied bravely to the cause, but essentially it was a cause in which he no longer believed. This is a point he confirmed in an interview with Tony Crawley of

122

Starburst magazine: 'The story that Han Solo was part of . . . is over. The story completes itself in this third film. I had a great time on *Return of the Jedi*. I'm glad I did it. I'm glad I did all three of them. But, as well, I'm glad . . . I don't have to do any more. After *Return of the Jedi* the saga goes back in time, so Solo's not in the next three. There will be nine films in all. Just three for Solo. I assume they will not replace me with another person to play Solo.'

The last line is significant: Ford may have felt a growing dis-association from the part, but it was essentially *his* creation, and he did not expect anyone else to be allowed to usurp it. What is perhaps more important is the sense of dissatisfac-tion that ran through the interview; it was as if Ford knew just how disappointing *Return of the Jedi* proved to be. Not even cuddly bears in a tree-lined space village can save an essentially mediocre film.

Of all the adverse critical comment aimed at the film, that of the American magazine *Variety* best summed up the general attitude: 'Harrison Ford, who was such an essential element of the first two outings, is present more in body than in spirit this time, given little to do but react to special effects.' In a sense, Ford had simply outgrown the part: Lucas' films appeal to the child in all of us, but even children's tastes change and develop in a way that Lucas' trilogy failed to do. The mythical quality of *Star Wars* became diluted to the level of a fairy tale in *Return of the Jedi*, and its essentially virtuous but flawed characters metamorphosed into goody-goody caricatures of themselves. Even Lucas seemed ready to acknowledge that the *Star Wars* myth had become self-perpetuating, had outgrown his or anyone's abilities to con-trol its intricacies. 'I'm tired of painting Sistine Chapels,' he told Dale Pollock. 'I'd rather go back to little four-by-four can-vases.'

123

The *Star Wars* trilogy was finally brought to a close, and the sense of completion was accompanied by a feeling of relief. At a time when he was under contract to nothing but the next *Raiders* film, Harrison Ford delighted in telling Dale Pollock: 'Massa George says ah kin go at the end of eighty-five – a freed man!' His tone may have been humorous, but his underlying concern was apparent. Perhaps, despite himself, Ford had allowed himself to become yoked to the dreams and ambitions of another. Even when that other is as close and gifted a friend as George Lucas, the effect can be disenchanting. The success of Ford's career was enhanced by the continuing legend of *Star Wars*, but the diversity he sought as an actor was not. *Return of the Jedi* relied on the faith of its audience for its success, whereas *Star Wars* had inspired that faith. Though Harrison Ford rallied bravely to the cause, it was essentially a cause in which he no longer believed.

Needless to say, the audience disagreed: Jedi proved to be the third most profitable film of all time, and was hailed by Lucas fans as the perfect ending to the *Star Wars* adventure.

9

The Hero is Back

After the relative disappointment of *Return of the Jedi*, Harrison Ford was, ironically, to find great satisfaction from yet another sequel to a George Lucas film, the massively successful *Raiders of the Lost Ark*. But before he could turn his attention to that, there were other, more personal matters to clear up.

In February 1983 his final divorce papers from Mary came through, and he was free to marry Melissa Matheson. On 14 March 1983 he did so – very quietly. Perhaps because his first marriage had failed as an almost direct consequence of his elevation to stardom, Ford had no wish to place his second on public view. Melissa Matheson was heavily involved in the film business herself, so the pressures might well have been dissipated by common experience, but Ford was taking no chances. 'All the fame after *Star Wars* killed my first marriage,' he observed. 'I want life with Melissa to be as private as possible. The only spotlight I want is when I am making a movie. We live as quietly as possible, and that's the way we were married.'

There was no elaborate honeymoon either. Both returned home after the wedding, he to work in the garden, she to continue writing one of the many scripts she had in the pipeline. For ninety-nine per cent of the world, Harrison Ford had stopped being ordinary a long time before, but he was not going to let go so easily. It was soon time to get back to the world of film, however.

Ford was cast as Eliot's headmaster in *E.T.* and filmed a brief ten-minute sequence for the film, but on the final cut it was felt that the little coterie of Ford, Matheson – who was the script writer on the film – and Spielberg was just a little too cosy for comfort. Then the Big Time beckoned once again.

Ford had known for some months that Lucas' latest offering, *Indiana Jones and the Temple of Doom*, was ready to be set in production, and he had in fact signed up for that film and the inevitable 'Indy III', already plotted but as yet untitled. Once again, Lucas had managed to inveigle Steven Spielberg to agree to direct, or as Spielberg himself put it: 'I wanted to do it because I didn't want someone to do a better job than I did on *Raiders*, all of which suited Harrison Ford perfectly. During *Raiders of the Lost Ark* he and Spielberg had developed one of the closest professional relationships that the sycophantic world of Hollywood would allow.

'This is very exciting for me,' he told Alan McKenzie. 'It was one of the best working relationship experiences of my life working with Steven.' More than that, perhaps, the two of them had the unerring ability to translate George Lucas' sometimes indeterminate ideas into convincing action on-screen. Spielberg himself acknowledged Ford's contribution in the television special *The Making of Indiana Jones and the Temple of Doom*. 'The character had just been thinly drawn on paper, a character who was defined by his heroics and by his sort of 'jungle-smarts', he observed. 'What Harrison did was to bring the character of Indiana Jones to life.'

This was an ability that would be sorely needed in *Temple of Doom*, for Lucas had decided that this film was going to have everything, and then some: 'Indy can do anything,' he told *Rolling Stone* magazine. 'He's a lot of thirties heroes put together. . . In some stories we'll see him in top hat and tails.

126

We don't want to make him Superman – he's just open to all possibilities. *Raiders* is the most action-oriented of the Indiana Jones movies – the others should deal more with the occult.'

The most obvious problem about *Temple of Doom* was the need to avoid the pressing temptation merely to reprise the role, having Indy repeat the same acts of high drama and heroics in front of a changing backdrop. Harrison Ford had done so much with the character in the first film that there was not a great range of possibilities left to extend it. The temptation to sit back and enjoy it was not entirely to be avoided.

Before such problems could be faced, however, George Lucas had to find himself a writer, and this time he could not get his first choice. Lawrence Kasdan, who had proved so successful in scripting *Raiders*, *Empire* and *Jedi* for him was now riding that success: he had already written and directed the wonderful *Body Heat* (co-incidentally starring Kathleen Turner, who was to star in the only decent film to follow in the wake of *Raiders – Romancing the Stone*), and was now doing the same on *The Big Chill*. This time Lucas was out of luck. For the first time since success had come his way, Lucas found his original choice for a member of cast or crew declining his offer. In response, he turned to tried-and-tested colleagues Gloria Katz and Willard Huyck, who had come up with the final and only workable script for *American Graffiti*. This film was rapidly turning into a class of 'seventy-two reunion.

Harrison Ford was satisfied with Lucas' choices in every department. Although never putting less than one hundred per cent of his energies into a part, the more faith he had in the background staff, the more relaxed he could be in his role. Unfortunately, he was to become perhaps a little too relaxed. His initial feelings were more than positive, however.

'I tell you, this movie's got even more action than the last one,' he told William Hall. 'There's a fight on a runaway train down a mine-shaft, a chase in the back alleys of Macao, snakes, spiders – you name it, we've done it.'

Perhaps the fact that there was so much in the film made it simply spill over. It provided far too much of a once-excellent thing. Many of the problems could be traced to the way the script was put together. In an extended interview with *Starlog* magazine, Lawrence Kasdan detailed some of the scenes which he, Lucas and Spielberg had decided to leave out of *Raiders*: 'In 1936 Shanghai was a battleground between the Japanese and the Chinese. General Hok was such an outlaw, though, that he was *aligned* with the Japanese. I had Indy being taken to Hok's museum by two CIA agents. Indy then broke into the museum where he saw a complicated alarm system, part of which was a ten-foot-diameter gong. . . Naturally he set off the gong alarm. Hok came running into the room holding a sub-machine gun, which he then started firing at Indy. Indy managed to push the gong off its hook and then rolled it across the floor, running behind it, using it as a shield.' He also envisioned the idea of Indy bailing out of the 'plane in a life raft, which he then inflates and rides down the slope of the mountain to the Ravenwood saloon, but, he said, 'we took that scene out because we thought it would be too unbelievable'.

Katz and Huyck, however, clearly felt these ideas were too good to waste, and incorporated them into their script for *Temple of Doom*. The gong sequence worked well enough, but the scene with the life raft was as unbelievable as Kasdan had feared. Not even Indiana Jones was *that* lucky. The tendency towards the unbelievable that *Raiders* had so deftly avoided – it is only after you come out of the cinema that you realize just

128

how unlikely the story premise actually is – was not to be re-sisted this time. Where *Raiders* had relied on spectacular stunts, *Temple of Doom* was going to rely merely on the specta-cular. It was a short-sighted view that would sorely damage the film's overall presentation.

The two writers actually spent only sixteen weeks coming up with three differently worked scripts for the film – a fast pace even by Hollywood standards – and it was perhaps be-cause of the pressures that such a race against time gave rise to that they felt the need to look to the original story for in-spiration. It is surprising, considering what a perfectionist Lucas is, that such a situation was allowed to arise. It all pointed to a lack of care, and an undue amount of haste, both uncharacteristic of the Ford-Lucas-Spielberg triumvirate. Observers hoped that this was not a sign of growing com-placency, of their belief that they could put less effort into the film and yet still make it as successful as its predecessor. Only time would tell.

In late 1982, with all the preliminary work completed and a script under their belts, the Lucasfilm entourage began to scout locations for *Temple of Doom*. The predominant flavour of the adventures this time was to be Far Eastern, and the team quickly decided upon Macao on the coast of South China as a passable imitation for Shanghai, where the film's opening sequence was set. From there they went to Sri Lanka, where they discovered areas which they could use for the scenes which supposedly take place in India. In fact, they decided upon many of the same locations that had been used in *Bridge Over the River Kwai*. They had initially planned a minimal shoot in India itself, but had met with government attempts to censor the script; attempts which Lucas in part-icular was not prepared to sanction. So India was out.

After the foreign locations had been decided upon, a few studio sets had to be built, the Maharajah's palace in particular, and for that they chose the familiar environs of Elstree. By the time *Temple of Doom* was finished, Harrison Ford had become such a regular visitor to the pubs in Borehamwood, that the locals knew him by his first name, and were refreshingly unimpressed by his presence amongst them. Both the familiarity of the surroundings, and the fact that many of the crew used on the film were those employed on *Raiders* would contribute to a remarkably easy shooting schedule.

Now that Spielberg knew where he was going to shoot, he had to decide just who was going to be there when he was doing it. He had known for some time that Karen Allen had decided not to repeat her role as Marion Ravenwood, so if there was to be any romantic involvement this time a different actress would have to be found. After checking out dozens, if not hundreds of possibles – both discreetly, and more overtly at auditions – Spielberg decided to utilize the talents of Kate Capshaw. Capshaw was about as different from Karen Allen as it was possible to be; from appearance to mannerisms, to the way she came across on-screen. Her shock of blonde hair and wide-eyed, almost empty-headed innocence counter-pointed Allen's dark, determined and knowing Marion Ravenwood. This would clearly shift the points of emphasis in Harrison Ford's portrayal of Indiana Jones. It did not augur well.

For the time-being, however, casting continued. In this film Indy was to have more than one partner: Wu Han, played by David Yip; and Short Round, played by the inimitable Ke Huy Quan, a Vietnamese refugee whose glorious acting shone through the film, and who went on to star in Spielberg's *The Goonies*. Wu Han gets shot very early in the film,

130

which is interesting because it is the only example thus far of Indy's adventures bringing death to those close to him, and indicative of the way in which *Temple of Doom* was intended to be a far less cosy film than *Raiders* had been. For the principal villain, Mola Ram, Spielberg lighted upon Amrish Puri, a leading actor in India whose ability to gaze balefully at Jones was enough to make anyone stick their head under the blankets. Perhaps because of some ill-judged criticisms at the time of *Star Wars*, it seemed Lucas was determined to make this an overtly multi-racial film. He may also have felt his conscience pricked by the fact he had shied away from casting a black actor as Han Solo in that earlier film. He felt he was not going to make the same mistake twice.

Unfortunately he did. On its release the film was criticized for the roles apportioned to the ethnic members of the cast. These were roles in which their practices and customs were ridiculed. The banquet scene, where live monkeys' brains are consumed, seemed particularly derogatory, and it is difficult to imagine why Lucas, and indeed Ford let this kind of idea through.

Once the remaining parts had been cast, *Temple of Doom* was set in motion on 18 April 1983. Harrison Ford, married only thirty-five days, found himself first in Macao and then Sri Lanka, on an exotic honeymoon all by himself. And he had some unusual companions. . .

When George Lucas originally rang Ford to explain about the film, the actor reputedly said, 'I don't mind what we do George, but I think we should have elephants'. And elephants they had, though things did not go exactly as planned for Harrison Ford. 'We've got a whole bunch of them,' he told William Hall, 'and I have to fight a battle on their backs. Those brutes are harder to ride than camels, and

I've had experience of both. They sway all over the place. If they shift one way and you're going the other, that's it, brother. You're in the dust.' And so was Harrison Ford. On one occasion he fell so badly that he found himself with constant back pain, reactivating an old complaint that had first arisen in adolescence, and that had been aggravated by his car crash in 1966. After being examined by the location doctor, it was decided that he should return to the United States for laser surgery. The process took a good three weeks to complete, and Spielberg had to shoot around him without knowing when – or if – he would return.

Fortunately Ford suffered no permanent damage, primarily because he was in such good shape. Though resolutely anti physical fitness in the Hollywood cult sense of the phrase, the adventures he had to perform for *Temple of Doom* were so strenuous that he had undergone a period of training with bodybuilder to the Stars Jake. (When you have got a body like this man, you only need one name). As Spielberg observed to *Rolling Stone* magazine, 'He's like a coach. . . Jake fills you with the feeling of mind over matter.' It was fortunate the director had managed to convince Ford of Jake's talents: without preliminary physical fitness training, he might have found the accident significantly more debilitating. Ford was suitably chastized by this lesson, and though he was not convinced of the efficacy of the jogging craze *et al* – 'I've never seen a happy jogger,' he once observed – he now puts in a little regular effort to maintain the level of fitness gained for *Temple of Doom*.

After twelve weeks of hectic shooting at Elstree Studios, the production moved back to California to shoot the final segment of the rope-bridge scene, and then, on 8 September 1983, the further adventures of Indiana Jones were sealed in the can. Paramount decided upon the slogan 'The Hero is Back' to inform a breathlessly waiting world that Indiana Jones would be coming to tea in the very near future. Royal premieres were arranged; the Prince and Princess of Wales arrived at the Empire Leicester Square to meet Steven Spielberg, though Harrison Ford avoided the razzamatazz, and everyone decided this film was going to be bigger than World War Two. Then everything went wrong.

First of all, there was the problem with cuts. *Temple of Doom* proved to be a film about death and mayhem, all of which may be good clean fun in the appropriate setting, but it did not work this time. The camera seemed to linger just a little too long over the scenes of torture; so much so that, in the un-cut original press showing, even hardened old critics found the portrayal of Mola Ram plucking a still-beating heart from his victim's chest just a little too realistic. In response, the film met with a PG certificate in America, a level of censorship many still found too liberal, and one with which the British Board of Film Censors disagreed. If the American print was to be released in this country, they observed, it would inevitably meet with an adults-only '18' rating. Paramount in particular were horrified by the suggestion, for much of the film's envisaged profitability had been calculated on the basis of an adolescent and younger audience, and they agreed to many significant cuts in order to bring the film down to what they considered a suitable level of certification.

It was indeed a violent film. But it was not the first such one in which Spielberg had been involved. The remarkable, if at times gruesome *Poltergeist* had its public performances in the States marked by mothers, who had clearly expected something cute and cuddly, taking their bemused children home early. There was a similarly disconcerting quality about

133

Temple of Doom; an underlying feeling that its creators were revelling in the distaste and horror the film engendered in its audience. Harrison Ford disagreed fundamentally with this and similar observations: 'It's a movie in which evil, in all its nasty and unpleasant forms, is defeated by the power of good', he commented. Spielberg similarly leaped to the defence, noting in the *Making of Indiana Jones* television documentary that, 'There are some scenes that are violent and depict the evil of the Temple of Doom. This picture is not called "The Temple of Rose" – it's called *The Temple of Doom*. The warning is clearly marked on the box.' Unfortunately that was not the problem. It was the nasty aftertaste left by the chocolates that bothered most people.

Violence aside, the film was revealed as failing in the most unforgivable fashion, when seen in relation to *Raiders of the Lost Ark*: it simply did not make sense. George Lucas had decided to make it a 'prequel', a Hollywood phrase used to describe a film set some time before the original. It was a decision that had caused many problems, and not all of them were faced squarely enough. Harrison Ford himself observed on the television special that, 'They pulled a little trick on me – they made him two or three years younger than he was last time. I don't know why they would do something like that, because I got three years older and the character got two years younger, which makes me five years older than I should be for the character. And I can feel the difference.'

Apart from creating Ford's difficulty in assimilating the change in his character's age, the use of the prequel ploy opened up significant gaps in the plot. For example, in *Raiders* Indiana Jones mocks his boss, Marcus Brody, for believing the Ark of the Covenant may have some kind of special power. He says, 'I don't believe in magic, a lot of superstitious hocus-pocus. I'm going after a find with incredible historical significance. You're talking about the bogeyman' – all of which fitted into place in the original, but which was totally rebutted by Indy's experience in the second film. In *Temple of Doom* he makes active use of magic, chanting in a fashion that makes the Sankara stones become searing hot to Mola Ram's touch. This is more than a simple oversight, it is a fundamental change in the character of Indiana Jones, and one that is never explained or even referred to in the course of the action. It points to a lack of care and attention to detail that is uncharacteristic of those involved on the film, especially Harrison Ford.

Perhaps worst of all is the fact that *Temple of Doom* slips into the trap of belittling women. The character of Willie Scott, as played by Kate Capshaw and devised by Steven Spielberg, becomes a helpless, laughable woman, who survives only with the help of her hunky companion. She is scared of insects; finds elephants horrible, smelly things which she tries to render less offensive by the application of perfume; and she clumsily nearly sentences Jones and Short Round to death. The attempted seduction scene is less insulting than positively distasteful. Throughout it all, Jones becomes a macho boor. In *Raiders* he was a rounded, flawed character.

It was as if Spielberg had chosen to work out all his least savoury ideas in the context of a film he knew could not fail. He has always professed a desire to film one of the James Bond features, and unfortunately in *Temple of Doom* it was a desire that became all too visible. Ford seemed to be manipulated into playing a role that owed more to the inconsequential adventure films of the early seventies than to the old Republic studio's serials. Sadly, Ford seemed to take to the part just a little too readily.

135

Indiana Jones and the Temple of Doom is the most disappointing of Harrison Ford's films so far. This is a judgement based not so much on quality, for taken by itself it is better than ninety per cent of the films released in that year, but because it fails to match the standards set by Ford's performance in *Raiders of the Lost Ark*.

Needless to say, the rest of the world disagreed. On its release in 1984, *Temple of Doom* very nearly imitated its predecessor's performance, and it reached number two in the film charts, being edged out only by the wonderfully crackpot *Ghostbusters*. After the Royal Premiere in London crowds queued for three hours, snaking round the block, to see the first public showing. Afterwards they gave the film a near-standing ovation. They liked it.

Harrison Ford, meanwhile, was ready to hang his hat and bullwhip away for a while. He wanted to turn his attention elsewhere.

10

And Finally . . .

After twenty-two years in the acting business Harrison Ford arrived at precisely the destination he had originally set himself. Even amongst those he regarded as completely antithetical to the spirit of film-making, he was regarded as a capable and versatile actor; one able to apply his talents successfully to any task that presented itself. But following the enormous, if imitative success of *Indiana Jones and the Temple of Doom*, there was nowhere else for him to go but sideways. There was simply no way in which he could duplicate the kind of success that Indiana Jones had brought his way; the character and circumstances of the production were simply too individual for that to be possible. He realized immediately that his future had to lie in films in which he could explore more subtle modes of acting.

He had to face the problem that was imposed by the image of Harrison Ford, on-screen hero, that was presented to the world at large. Many people seemed to see him strictly in terms of the characters he played: heroic in a curious sense, and a star, definitively so. It was a mantle he showed no readiness to wear. 'I just try to be as normal as possible and keep to myself, away from the crowd,' he told William Hall. 'I don't appear in public too often, but the life I live is the best I can imagine. I'm not drawn to opulence, anyway. There'd be no pleasure for me to be living in Bel-Air.'

Perhaps because of that attitude, Ford has never fitted

comfortably into the Hollywood niche, his attendance at the annual George Lucas Independence Day celebrations is about as social as he gets. That may be why many of the parts that came his way after *Temple of Doom* were not the usual type to arrive on the desk of a man with such a high-profile acting persona. His pedigree as a student of serious, and not so serious acting may be impeccable on reflection, but Hollywood executives tend to see only as far as the dollar signs in the foyer. Fortunately Ford is one actor they were not able to pigeon-hole.

Immediately after the end of *Temple of Doom* Ford chose to return to Melissa for a while, and informed his agent that he was temporarily unavailable for work. He felt he had some home life to catch up on, and he wanted to spare some time for Ben and Willard, over whom he and Mary had joint custody. Thus, for a few months at the end of 1984, he became a bit of a recluse, at least by Bel-Air standards. He still mingled with the same film people he had always done, however: Steven Spielberg and his girlfriend, George Lucas and his wife Marcia, remained frequent companions outside the professional milieu that had brought them together.

It was interesting to see how the three men extended their involvement with each other beyond the making of films. Each of them saw in the others a reflection of his own perspective and attitudes – to life as well as film.

All of them appreciated the problems encapsulated by Lucas in an interview with *Rolling Stone*, when he observed: 'Part of the problem is that success has made it so that I don't have any life of my own. . . You end up not being happy any more and working yourself to death.' By keeping in close contact with one another the Ford-Lucas-Spielberg trio were able to avoid the worst of that pressure. Harrison Ford in particular, with one failed marriage behind him already, was grateful for the protection.

Ford was not prepared to sit on his laurels for too long, however. Out of the plethora of scripts that he had dutifully read through, he decided upon a picture in which his role would be one of underplaying rather than exaggerating his on-screen presence. He saw it in nice juxtaposition to the role of Indiana Jones, whose spectacular heroics followed him everywhere. Now it was time to play someone who made simple mistakes again.

The story he chose involved a Philadelphia detective investigating a murder that inadvertently involves the Amish people, a Dutch Reform sect who believe in eschewing progress and the modern world. Originally entitled *Believers*, the film was changed to *Witness*, an alteration that indicates the shift in emphasis that the script revisions brought about from the original idea. From being a rather ill-defined study of a group of people who exist in a quasi time-bubble, it became an exploration of the effect on an individual of the modern world he has witnessed through its worst vice. The use of an Amish child successfully conveys the notion of openness and impressionability, whilst Harrison Ford's hardened John Book perfectly captures the way in which a modern individual, on entering an old-fashioned world, finds his prejudices and beliefs turned inside out.

One of the most dramatic scenes in the film is the spectacular barn-building sequence, which was in part suggested and developed by Harrison Ford during the many script conferences involved with the production. It was the perfect on-screen exposition of the blend of carpenter and actor that was Harrison Ford, and he revelled fully in its playing out. He had convinced director Peter Weir that the scene should be given significant importance because the craft of woodworking was one which connected both the old world and the new. The fact that it did the same for the actor was not merely coincidental. During the times when the film world had been less than convinced of his abilities as an actor, he had regained his self-esteem and sense of perspective, and not a little remuneration, through his carpentry.

The production was centred principally on location in the United States, which was another positive factor influencing Ford's decision to take the part, and most of the shooting took place in the mid-West which Ford knew so well. There was something about mid-America, an honesty and an openness, a no-nonsense attitude which impressed him. His expressed aversion to bullshit was well-catered for here.

Director Peter Weir, an Australian whose track record included the haunting *Picnic at Hanging Rock* and *Gallipoli*, saw the film as an opportunity to confirm his status in Hollywood, but he also had a sense of film-making that went beyond the simple dollar fixation of many of his business partners. He was also looking forward to working with Harrison Ford for the first time. 'I knew Harrison was pretty much set for the part when I took the job,' he observed, 'and I'd obviously seen his work before. I particularly liked him in *Blade Runner* – so I was excited at the idea of making a movie with him.' Ford, similarly, knew of Weir's previous films, and quickly struck up a productive partnership with him. 'Peter Weir is a director who knows what he's doing,' he noted. 'I like that.' The production of *Witness* also gave rise to the kind of family feel that had characterized Ford's previous films with George Lucas and Steven Spielberg. He liked that as well.

The film allowed Ford the kind of romantic involvement with a co-star that only *Hanover Street* had hinted at before.

(Carrie Fisher might have described Ford enthusiastically as 'a great kisser' during the filming of *The Empire Strikes Back*, but even the most ardent *Star Wars* fan had to admit that Han Solo and the Princess never really 'got it on'). Kelly McGillis, the Amish woman who finds John Book is more than just a symbol of the outside world, matches Ford perfectly, and the emotional chemistry that they generate on-screen adds a dimension to Ford's playing that had not been seen before.

In some ways *Witness* seemed a curious project for Harrison Ford to become involved in. Though by no means a B-movie – and in this age of escalating budgets, that format is a luxury Hollywood can no longer afford – it certainly seemed to be a lesser light, retreating behind the overtly spectacular blockbuster movies set for release the same year. Ford had no doubt about his involvement in such a film, however. 'I do enjoy doing the physical stuff,' he told William Hall, 'though, to be honest, I'm not particularly brave myself. I've been inundated with action scripts ever since I got into the mould. Hollywood follows a successful trail ot footprints, doesn't it? But there comes a point where you become independently bankable, where they want you for things that aren't just one type of slam-bang role – and I'm glad to say I seem to have reached that point at last. People know that I want to do other things now.'

It is clear that Ford was nailing his colours to the mast, declaring once and for all that he was an actor who was more than just Superman without the red tights. This time, he was more successful than in his previous attempt, immediately following *Star Wars*. Perhaps because he avoided rushing into the need to prove himself, or even because his personal life was so much more stable and fulfilling, his involvement with *Witness* worked in every way.

141

That it worked was recognized by Ford's peers in the film business. Both film and actor were nominated for Oscars and, though Ford found the carnival atmosphere often associated with the ceremony antithetical to everything he believed in, he communicated an underlying sense of satisfaction at having finally shown that Columbia official in 1963 just how wrong he had been.

Harrison Ford is now one of the most adept and sought-after cinema actors in the world; at the time of the announcement that Roger Moore would no longer be taking the role of James Bond, it was rumoured that Ford was being considered for the part. He had not attained this level of respect and popularity single-handed, however. Directors George Lucas and Steven Spielberg, whose refreshing approach to film-making caused them to be dubbed 'The Movie Brats', were more than instrumental in his success. Part of the reason that they too have been so successful is that both have the ability to infuse new ideas with traditional values on-screen. And part of that moral tradition has been most succinctly represented by Harrison Ford.

The work the three men undertook together used Hollywood machinery without ever letting money enter the equation. The combination of their personalities offered a perfect blend of idealism, practicality and visual invention. Lucas believed in an almost esoteric quality of film; Harrison Ford saw it all as a job worth doing; and Steven Spielberg had the ability to bring it all simply but individually to cinematic life. As Lucas told *Rolling Stone* magazine when asked about Spielberg: 'He's the perfect director for me to work with. We just think the same way about everything. He'll go a little overboard one way, and I'll go overboard another way, but there's no conflict. . . He keeps saying it's my movie and I'll get blamed for it, and I keep saying it's his movie and he'll get blamed for it.'

Into this finely balanced relationship walked Harrison Ford, who succeeded in bringing the best out of both, where others would have perhaps been overawed by the peculiar symbiosis of the two men. Ford's involvement in the *Star Wars* trilogy was fundamental to its success; as Indiana Jones he was the personification of what Lucas and Spielberg had envisioned. In a sense, Ford, Lucas and Spielberg have succeeded in creating an alternative Hollywood. Seperately, all remain successful, but together they are simply unassailable. Ford, for example, has appeared many times in films scheduled to be blockbusters – particularly *Blade Runner* – which, though gaining honourable mentions, fall short of expectations. Somehow he has yet to demonstrate that peculiar chemistry when away from his mentors that he so perfectly achieves when working with them. Perhaps he remains wary of everybody else in the business, and is never able to give quite a hundred per cent to others.

The quality of performance Ford has brought to the Lucas-Speilberg partnership is best summed up by Spielberg himself in the *Temple of Doom* television special: 'Harrison's ideas are really good, and I'll listen to his ideas, and he might have a way of doing something, and that might give *me* an idea, and I might re-double his idea and think of an even better way to do something, and Harrison might then even top that with another way to do something.'

In short, Harrison Ford is an actor who brings to his films an extra dimension, even intuition; he knows exactly what will and will not work at any given moment. Once he can perfectly exercise that ability independently of Lucas and Spielberg he can honestly be described as the perfect star for the eighties.

Meanwhile, he continues to enjoy his work. 'The day I don't, that's when I'll give it all up,' he has observed. And for Harrison Ford you can safely say that day will never come.

Filmography

Dead Heat on a Merry-Go-Round (1966)

Starring James Coburn (*Eli Kotch*), Camilla Sparv (*Inger Knudson*), Aldo Ray (*Eddie Hart*), Nina Wayne (*Frieda Schmid*), Robert Webber (*Milo Stewart*), Rose Marie (*Margaret Kirby*), Todd Armstrong (*Alfred Morgan*), Marian Moses (*Dr Marion Hague*), Michael Strong (*Paul Feng*), Severn Darden (*Miles Fisher*), James Westerfield (*Jack Balter*), Philip E.Pine (*George Logan*), Simon Scott (*William Anderson*), Ben Astar (*General Mailenkoff*), Lawrence Mann (*Officer Howard*), Michael St.Angel (*Captain William Yates*), Alex Rodine (*Translator*), Albert Nalbandian (*Willie Manus*), Tyler McVey (*Lyman Mann*), Roy Glenn (*Sergeant Elmer K.Coxe*), Harrison Ford (*Bellboy*).
Directed by Bernard Girard, Screenplay by Bernard Girard, Photographed by Lionel Linden, Edited by William Lyon, Art direction by Walter M. Simonds, Music by Stu Phillips, Produced by Carter De-Haven.

Luv (1967)

Starring Jack Lemmon (*Harry Berlin*), Peter Falk (*Milt Manville*), Elaine May (*Ellen*), Nina Wayne (*Linda*), Eddie Mayehoff (*Attorney Goodhart*), Paul Martman (*Doyle*), Severn Darden (*Vandergrist*), and Harrison Ford.
Directed by Clive Donner, Screenplay by Elliott Baker, based on the play by Murray Schisgal, Photographed by Ernest Laszlo, Produced by Martin Manulis.

The Long Ride Home (1967, aka: A Time For Killing)

Starring Glenn Ford (*Major Walcott*), George Hamilton (*Captain Bentley*), Inger Stevens (*Emily Biddle*), Paul Petersen (*Blue Lake*), Max Baer (*Sgt Luther Liskell*), Todd Armstrong (*Lt Prudessing*), Timothy Carey (*Billy Cat*), Kenneth Toby (*Sgt Cleehan*), Richard X. Slattery (*Corp Paddy Darling*), Duke Hobbie (*Lt Frist*), Dean Stanton (*Sgt Dan Way*), James Davidson (*Little Mo*), Harrison J. Ford (*Lt Shaffer*), Charlie Briggs (*Sgt Kettlinger*), Kay E. Kuter (*Owelson*), Dick Miller (*Zollic officer*), Craig Curtis (*Bagnef*), Emile Miller (*Col Harries*), Marshall Reed (*Stedner*), Jay Ripley (*Lovingwood*), Dean Goodhill (*Bruce*).
Directed by Phil Carlson, Screenplay by Halsted Welles, based on the novel *Southern Blade* by Nelson and Shirly Wolford, Photographed by Kenneth Peach, Edited by Roy Livingston, Music by Mundell Lowe, Produced by Harry Joe Brown.

Journey to Shiloh (1967)

Starring James Caan (*Buck Burnett*), Michael Sarrazin (*Miller Nalls*), Brenda Scott (*Gabrielle Du Prey*), Don Stroud (*Todo McLean*), Paul Petersen (*J.C. Sutton*), Michael Burns (*Eubi Bell*), Michael Vincent (*Little Bit Buck*), Harrison Ford (*Willie Bill Beardon*), John Doucette (*Gen Braxton Bragg*).
Directed by William Hale, Screenplay by Gene Coon based on the novel *Fields of Honour* by Will Henry, Photographed by Enzo A. Martinelli, Produced by Howard Christie.

Getting Straight (1970)

Starring Elliott Gould (*Harry Bailey*), Candice Bergen (*Jan*), Robert F. Lyons (*Nick*), Jeff Corey (*Dr Wilhunt*), Max Julien (*Ellis*), Cecil Kellaway (*Dr Kasper*), John Lormer (*Vandenburg*), Leonard Stone (*Lysander*), William Bramley (*Wade Linden*), Jeannie Berlin (*Judy Kramer*), John Rubenstein (*Herbert*), Richard Anders (*Dr Greengrass*), Brenda Sykes (*Luan*), Jenny Sullivan (*Sheila*), Gregory Sierra (*Garcia*), Billie Bird (*Landlady*), Harrison Ford (*Jake*), Elizabeth Lane (*Alice Linden*), Hilarie Thompson (*Cynthia*), Irene Tedrow (*Mrs Stebbins*),

Joanna Serpe (*Room-mate*), Scott Perry (*Airline Representative*).
Directed by Richard Rush, Screenplay by Robert Kaufman, based on the novel by Ken Kolb, Photographed by Lazlo Kovacs, Edited by Maury Winetrobe, Produced by Richard Rush.

American Graffiti (1973)

Starring Richard Dreyfuss (*Curt*), Ron Howard (*Steve*), Paul Le Mat (*John*), Charles Martin Smith (*Terry the Toad*), Cindy Williams (*Laurie*), Candy Clark (*Debbie*), Mackenzie Phillips (*Carol*), Wolfman Jack (*Disc Jockey*), Harrison Ford (*Bob Falfa*), Bo Hopkins (*Joe*), Manuel Padilla (*Carlos*), Beau Gentry (*Ants*), Kathleen Quinlan (*Peg*), Suzanne Somers (*Blonde in T-Bird*), Debralee Scott (*Falfa's Girl*).
Directed by George Lucas, Screenplay by George Lucas, Gloria Katz and Willard Huyck, Photographed by Haskell Wexler, Ron Eveslage and Jan Dalquen, Edited by Verna Fields and Marcia Lucas, Sound and recording by Walter Murch, Casting by Fred Roos and Mike Fenton, Co-produced by Gary Kurtz, Prouduced by Francis Ford Coppola.

The Conversation (1974)

Starring Gene Hackman (*Harry Caul*), John Cazale (*Stan*), Allen Garfield (*Berni Moran*), Frederic Forrest (*Mark*), Cindy Williams (*Ann*), Michael Higgins (*Paul*), Elizabeth MacRae (*Meredith*), Terri Garr (*Amy*), Harrison Ford (*Martin Stett*), Mark Wheeler (*Receptionist*), Robert Shields (*Mime*), Phoebe Alexander (*Lurleen*), Robert Duvall (*The Director*).
Directed by Francis Ford Coppola, Screenplay by Francis Ford Coppola, Photographed by Bill Butler, Edited by Walter Murch and Richard Chew, Music by David Shire, Produced by Francis Ford Coppola and Fred Roos.

Dynasty (1976, TV Movie)

Starring Sarah Miles (*Jennifer Blackwood*), Stacey Keach (*Matt Black-*

(handwritten annotations:)
1968
5 court martial of Lt Calley
6 The Possessed 1968
7 Zabrieski point 1969

wood), Harris Yulin (*John Blackwood*), Harrison Ford (*Mark Black-wood*), Tony Schwartz (*Harry Blackwood*), Amy Irving (*Amanda Blackwood*), Charles Weldon (*Sam Adams*), Stephanie Faulkner (*Lucinda*), Karmin Murcello (*Elvira*), John Carter (*Benjamin McCullum*), Sari Price (*Margaret McCullum*), Gerrit Graham (*Carver Blackwood*), Dennis Larson (*Mark, age 12*), Gary Lee Cooper (*Mark, age 6*).

Directed by Lee Philips, Teleplay by Sydney Carroll, based on the novel by James Michener, Produced by Buck Houghton.

Star Wars (1977)

Strarring Mark Hamill (*Luke Skywalker*), Harrison Ford (*Han Solo*), Carrie Fisher (*Princess Leia Organa*), Peter Cushing (*Grand Moff Tarkin*), Sir Alec Guinness (*Ben "Obi-wan" Kenobi*), Anthony Daniels (*C-3PO*), Kenny Baker (*R2-D2*), Peter Mayhew (*Chewbacca*), David Prowse (*Lord Darth Vader*), Phil Brown (*Uncle Owen Lars*), Shelagh Fraser (*Aunt Beru Lars*), Jack Purvis (*Chief Jawa*), Biggs (*Dennis Lawson*).

Written and directed by George Lucas, Photographed by Gilbert Taylor, Edited by Paul Hirch, Marcia Lucas and Richard Chew, Production design by John Barry, Music by John Williams, Special effects supervisor John Dykstra, Sound effects by Ben Burtt, Production Supervisor Robert Watts, Produced by Gary Kurtz.

Heroes (1977)

Starring Henry Winkler (*Jack Dunne*), Sally Field (*Carol*), Harrison Ford (*Kenny Boyd*), Val Avery (*Bus Driver*), Olivia Cole (*Jan Adcox*), Hector Elias (*Dr Elias*), Dennis Burkley (*Gus*), Tony Burton (*Chef*), Michael Cavanaugh (*Peanuts*), Helen Craig (*Bus Depot Manager*), John P.Finnegan (*Mr Munro*), Betty McGuire (*Mrs Munro*), John O'Leary (*Ticket Clerk*), Tom Rosqui (*Second Patrolman*), Fred Struthman (*Nathan*), Caskey Swain (*Frank*), Earle Towne (*Leo Sturges*), Verna Bloom (*Waitress*), Kenneth Augustine (*Charles*), Rick Blanchard (*Andy*), Louis Carillo (*Stokes*), Robert Kretschman (*Robert*), Ledd Cohn (*Patient*), Dick Ziker (*Artie*).

Directed by Jeremy Paul Kagan, Screenplay by James Carabatsos,

Photographed by Frank Stanley, Edited by Patrick Kennedy, Music by Jack Nitzsche, Produced by David Foster and Lawrence Turman.

Force 10 from Navarone (1978)

Starring Robert Shaw (*Major Mallory*), Harrison Ford (*Lieutenant-Colonel Mike Barnsby*), Barbara Bach (*Maritza Petrovitch*, Edward Fox (*Sergeant "Milly" Miller*), Franco Nero (*Captain Radicek*), Carl Wethers (*Sergeant Walter Weaver*), Richard Kiel (*Captain Drazak*), Alan Badel (*Major Petrovitch*), Angus MacInnes (*Lieutenant Doug Reynolds*), Michael Byrne (*Major Schroeder*), Philip Latham (*Commander Jensen*), Peter Buntic (*Lieutenant Marko*), Michael Sheard (*Sergeant Bauer*), Leslie Schofield, Antony Langdon and Richard Hampton (*Interrogation Officers*), Paul Humpoletz (*Sergeant Bismark*), Dicken Ashworth (*Nolan*), Christopher Malcolm (*Rogers*), Nick Ellsworth (*Salvone*), Jonathan Blake (*Oberstein*), Roger Owen (*Blake*), Frances Mughan, Mike Sirett, Graham Crowther and Jim Dowdall (*Force 10 Team*).
Directed by Guy Hamilton, Screenplay by Robin Chapman from a story by Carl Forman, based on a novel by Alistair MacLean, Photographed by Christopher Challis, Music by Ron Goodwin, Produced by Oliver A.Unger, Executive producer Carl Foreman.

Hanover Street (1979)

Starring Harrison Ford (*David Halloran*), Lesley-Anne Down (*Margaret Sellinger*), Christopher Plummer (*Paul Sellinger*), Alec McCowen (*Major Trumbo*), Richard Maur (*2nd Lt Jerry Cimino*), Michael Sacks (*2nd Lt Martin Hyer*), Patsy Kensit (*Sarah Sellinger*), Max Wall (*Harry Pike*), Shane Rimmer (*Col Ronald Bart*), Keith Buckley (*Lt Wells*), Sherrie Hewson (*Phyllis*), Cindy O'Callaghan (*Paula*), Di Trevis (*Elizabeth*), Suzanne Bertish (*French Girl*), Keith Alexander (*Soldier in Barn*), Jay Benedict (*Corp Daniel Giler*), John Ratzenberger (*Sgt John Lucas*), Eric Stine (*Farrell*), Hugh Frazer (*Capt Harold Lester*), William Hootkins (*Beef*).
Directed by Peter Hyams, Screenplay by Peter Hyams, Photographed by David Watkin, Edited by James Mitchell, Music by John Barry, Associate producers Michael Rachmil and Harry Benn, Prod-

149

uced by Paul N. Lazarus III, Executive producer Gordon G.T. Scott.

The 'Frisco Kid (1979)

Starring Gene Wilder (*Avram Belinski*), Harrison Ford (*Tommy Lillard*), Rammon Bieri (*Mr Jones*), Val Bisloglio (*Chief Gray Cloud*), George Ralph DiCenzo (*Darryl Riggs*), Leo Fuchs (*Chief Rabbi*), Penny Peyser (*Rosalie*), William Smith (*Matt Diggs*), Jack Somack (*Samuel Bender*), Beege Barkett (*Sarah Mindl*), Shay Duffin (*O'Leary*), Walter Janowitz (*Old Amish Man*), Joe Kapp (*Monterano*), Clyde Kusatsu (*Mr Ping*), Cliff Pellow (*Mr Daniels*), Allan Rich (*Mr Bialik*), Henry Rowland (*1st Amish Farmer*), Vincent Schiavelli (*Brother Bruno*), John Steadman (*Booking Agent*), Ian Wolfe (*Father Joseph*), Steffen Zacharias (*Herschel Rosensheine*), Eda Reiss Medin (*Mrs Bender*), Tommy Lillard (*Sheriff*).
Directed by Robert Aldrich, Screenplay by Michael Elias and Frank Shaw, Photographed by Robert B. Hauser, Edited by Maury Winetrobe, Irving Rosenblum and Jack Horger, Music by Frank DeVol, Associate producer Melvin Dellar, Produced by Mace Neufeld, Executive producer Howard W. Koch Jr.

The Empire Strikes Back (1980)

Starring Mark Hamill (*Luke Sykwalker*), Harrison Ford (*Han Solo*), Carrie Fisher (*Princess Leia Organa*), Billy Dee Williams (*Lando Calrissian*), Anthony Daniels (*C-3PO*), Kenny Baker (*R2-D2*), Peter Mayhew (*Chewbacca*), Frank Oz (*Yoda*), Sir Alec Guinness (*Ben "Obiwan" Kenobi*), Jeremy Bulloch (*Boba Fett*), John Hollis (*Lando's Aide*), Jack Purvis (*Chief Ugnaught*), Des Webb (*Snow Creature*), Clive Revill (*Voice of the Emperor*), Kenneth Colley (*Admiral Piett*), Julian Glover (*General Veers*), Dennis Lawson (*Wedge*).
Directed by Irvin Kershner, Screenplay by Leigh Brackett and Lawrence Kasdan, from a story by George Lucas, Photographed by Peter Suschitsky, Production design by Norman Reynolds, Music by John Williams, Edited by Paul Hirsch, Special effects supervised by Brian Johnson and Richard Edlund, Associate producer Robert Watts, Produced by Gary Kurtz, Executive Producer George Lucas.

150

Raiders of the Lost Ark (1981)

Starring Harrison Ford (*Prof. Indiana Jones*), Karen Allen (*Marion Ravenwood*), Paul Freeman (*Belloq*), Ronald Lacey (*Toht*), John Rhys-Davies (*Sallah*), Denholm Elliot (*Brody*), Wolf Kahler (*Dietrich*), Anthony Higgins (*Gobler*), Alfred Molina (*Satipo*), Vic Tablian (*Barranca*), Don Fellows (*Col. Musgrove*), William Hootkins (*Maj Eaton*). Directed by Steven Spielberg, Screenplay by Lawrence Kasdan, from a story by George Lucas and Philip Kaufman, Photographed by Douglas Slocombe, Production designed by Norman Reynolds, Music by John Williams, Edited by Michael Kahn, Visual Effects supervised by Richard Edlund, Associate producer Robert Watts, Produced by Frank Marshall, Executive producers George Lucas and Howard Kazanjian.

Blade Runner (1982)

Starring Harrison Ford (*Rick Deckard*), Rutger Hauer (*Roy Batty*), Sean Young (*Rachael*), Edward James Olmos (*Gaff*), M. Emmet Walsh (*Bryant*), Daryl Hannah (*Pris*), William Sanderson (*Sebastian*), Brion James (*Leon*), Joe Turkel (*Tyrell*), Joanna Cassidy (*Zhora*), James Hong (*Chew*), Morgan Paull (*Holden*), Kimiro Hiroshige (*Cambodian Lady*), Carolyn DeMirjian (*Saleslady*), Robert Ozkazaki (*Sushi Master*), Hy Pyke (*Taffy Lewis*), Kevin Thompson (*Bear*), John Edward Allen (*Kaiser*).
Directed by Ridley Scott, Screenplay by Hampton Fancher and David Peoples, based on the novel *Do Androids of Electric Sheep* by Philip K.Dick, Photographed by Jordan Cronenweth, Production designed by Lawrence G.Paul, Music by Vangelis, Supervising editor Terry Rawlings, Special effects supervised by Douglas Trumbull, Richard Yuricich and David Dryer, Visual futurist Syd Mead, Associate producer Ivor Powell, Produced by Michael Deeley, Executive producers Brian Kelly and Hampton Fancher.

Return of the Jedi (1983)

Starring Mark Hamill (*Luke Sykwalker*), Harrison Ford (*Han Solo*),

Carrie Fisher (*Princess Leia Organa*), Billy Dee Williams (*Lando Calrissian*), Anthony Daniels (*C-3PO*), Peter Mayhew (*Chewbacca*), Sebastian Shaw (*Anakin Sykwalker/Darth Vader*), David Prowse and Bob Anderson (*Darth Vader*, Ian McDiarmid (*The Emperor*), Frank Oz (*Yoda*), James Earl Jones (*voice of Darth Vader*), Sir Alec Guinness (*Ben "Obi-wan" Kenobi*), Jeremy Bulloch (*Boba Fett*).
Directed by Richard Marquand, Screenplay by Lawrence Kasdan, based on a story by George Lucas, Photographed by Alan Hume, Production designed by Norman Reynolds, Music by John Williams, Edited by Sean Barton, Marcia Lucas and Duwayne Dunham, Special visual effects by Dennis Muren, Ken Ralston and Richard Edlund, Makeup and creature design by Phil Tippett and Stuart Freeborn, Sound design by Ben Burtt, Co-produced by Robert Watts and Jim Bloom, Produced by Howard Kazanjian, Executive producer George Lucas.

Indiana Jones and the Temple of Doom (1984)

Starring Harrison Ford (*Indiana Jones*) with Kate Capshaw. Directed by Steven Spielberg, Screenplay by Gloria Katz and Willard Huyck, based on a story by George Lucas, Photographed by Douglas Slocombe, Supervising editor Michael Kahn, Edited by Peter Pitt, Production designed by Elliot Scott, Special effects supervisor George Gibbs, Stunt arranger Vic Armstrong, Associate producer Kathleen Kennedy, Produced by Robert Watts, Executive producers George Lucas and Frank Marshall.

Witness (1985)

Starring Harrison Ford (*John Book*) with Kelly McGillis, Josef Sommer, Lukas Haas, Alexander Godunov.
Directed by Peter Weir, Screenplay by Earl Wallace and William Kelley, based on a story by William Kelley and Earl and Pamela Wallace, Photographed by John Seale, Edited by Thomas Noble, Production designed by Stan Jolley, Music by Maurice Jarre, Produced by Edward S. Feldman.

251 m ___ ___ ___
2__ Freddie
___ Working ___ __
___ ___ ___ ___
___ ___ ___ ___

29 Presumed Innocent ___
___ Regarding Henry ___
3__ Patriot ___
___ ___ ___ ___
___ ___ ___ ___
__ ___ ___ ___ 94